Ms. Rupinder Jeet Kaur
Dr. Manminder Kaur

A Study of Academic Achievement of Adolescents in relation to Parental Encouragement

A Study of Academic Achievement of Adolescents in relation to Parental Encouragement

Rupinder Jeet Kaur
Assistant Professor,
Guru Teg Bahadur Khalsa College, Dasuya, Punjab (India)

Dr. Manminder Kaur
Assistant Professor,
BCM College of Education, Ludhiana, Pubab (India)

Canadian Academic Publishing

2014

Copyright © 2014. Rupinder Jeet Kaur and Dr. Manminder Kaur

All rights reserved. This book or any portion thereof may not be reproduced or used in any manner whatsoever without the express written permission of the publisher except for the use of brief quotations in a book review or scholarly journal.

Price : $27.86

First Edition : 2014

ISBN : 978-1-926488-01-1

Publisher ISBN Prefix : 978-1-926488

ISBN Allotment Agency : Library and Archives Canada (Govt. of Canada)

Published & Printed by
Canadian Academic Publishing
81, Woodlot Crescent,
Etobicoke,
Toronto, Ontario, Canada.
Postal Code- M9W 6T3
Phone- +1 (647) 633 9712
http://www.canadapublish.com

Dedicated to Almighty God & Loving Parents

ACKNOWLEDGEMENT

"Words are the poor representative of sentiments". The drops of words are few, but the ocean of feelings of gratitude is deeper in my heart for those who proved themselves to be lampposts in the way of accomplishing my research project.

First of all I am greatly and whole heartedly thankful to the Almighty who put strength in me to do and to accomplish the research work successfully with patience and confidence even in so many adverse situations.

Next to God, comes my honorable Guide Dr. Manminder Kaur Assistant professor of B.C.M College of education, Ludhiana. My language feels weak to express my inner feelings of indebtedness towards her who put in her heart and soul to guide me in this problem and above his entire encouragement attitude, concrete suggestions, untiring efforts and nice and cooperative behavior.

I am thankful to library staff of different colleges for easy access to books and reference material. In my feeling of gratitude, I express thanks to all the principals, teachers and students of various schools who cooperated me in the collection of data for my study.

I am also thankful to my parents who always encouraged me when I got nervous during research.

Last but not the least, thanks to many authors who remained behind the scene but whose works have been consulted and referred in this research project. All may not be mentioned but none is forgotten.

Rupinder Jeet Kaur

CONTENTS

1. INTRODUCTION   1 – 12

    1.1 Meaning of adolescence   2
    1.2 Academic Achievement   4
    1.3 Parental Encouragement   8
    1.4 Statement of the problem   10
    1.5 Operational Definitions   11
    1.6 Objectives of the study   11
    1.7 Need and Significance of the Study   11
    1.8 Delimitation of the Study   12
    1.9 Statistical Techniques Used   12

2. REVIEW OF LITERATURE   13 – 26

    2.1 Related Studies of Study Habit   16
    2.2 Related Studies of Parental Encouragement   24
    2.3 Hypotheses of the Study   26

3. METHOD AND PROCEDURE   27 – 33

    3.1 Design of the Study   29
    3.2 Sample   29
    3.3 Tools Employed   30
    3.4 Description of the tools   30
    3.5 Procedure for Collecting the Data   33
    3.6 Statistical Techniques to be used   33

CONTENTS

4.	**ANALYSIS AND INTERPRETATION**	**34 – 49**
5.	**SUMMARY AND CONCLUSIONS**	**50 – 61**
	5.1 Introduction	51
	5.1.1 Adolescence	51
	5.1.2 Academic Achievement	53
	5.1.3 Parental Encouragement	55
	5.2 Statement of the Study	56
	5.3 Operational Definition	57
	5.4 Objectives	57
	5.5 Hypotheses	57
	5.6 Need and Importance	57
	5.7 Design of the Study	58
	5.8 Sample	58
	5.9 Tools Used	59
	5.10 Statistical Techniques Used	59
	5.11 Conclusions	59
	5.12 Educational Implications	59
	5.13 Suggestions for further research	61
BIBLIOGRAPHY		**62 – 69**

LIST OF TABLES

TABLE NO.	DESCRIPTION	PAGE NO.
3.1	Showing Breakup of Total Sample	30
3.2	Showing Scoring Procedure	31
3.3	Showing Percentile Norms Of Parental Encouragement Scale	32
4.1	Frequency Distribution of scores of Parental Encouragement of Adolescent Boys and Girls (N = 200)	36
4.2	showing Mean, Median, Standard Deviation, Skewness and Kurtosis of scores of Parental Encouragement of Adolescent Boys and Girls (N = 200)	36
4.3	Frequency Distribution of scores of Parental Encouragement of Adolescents (N = 200)	37
4.4	showing Mean, Median, Standard Deviation, Skewness and Kurtosis of scores of Parental Encouragement of Adolescents (N = 200)	38
4.5	Frequency Distribution of scores of Academic Achievement of Adolescent Boys and Girls (N = 200)	39
4.6	showing Mean, Median, Standard Deviation, Skewness and Kurtosis of scores of Academic Achievement of Adolescent Boys and Girls (N = 200)	39
4.7	Frequency Distribution of scores of Academic Achievement of Adolescents (N = 200	40
4.8	showing Mean, Median, Standard Deviation, Skewness and Kurtosis of scores of Academic Achievement of Adolescents (N = 200)	41
4.9	Significance of the Difference between Mean Scores of Parental Encouragement of Adolescent Boys and Girls	42
4.10	Significance of the Difference between Mean Scores of Academic Achievement of Adolescent Boys and Girls	43

4.11	Summary of Analysis of Variance for scores of Academic Achievement of Adolescents with High, Average and Low Parental Encouragement	44
4.12	Showing the Mean Scores of Academic Achievement of Adolescents with High, Average and Low Parental Encouragement	44
4.13	Summary of Analysis of Variance for Scores of Academic Achievement of Adolescent Boys with High, Average and Low Parental Encouragement	45
4.14	Showing the Mean Scores of Academic Achievement of Adolescent Boys with High, Average and Low Parental Encouragement	45
4.15	Summary of Analysis of Variance for Scores of Academic Achievement of Adolescent Girls with High, Average and Low Parental Encouragement	46
4.16	Showing the Mean Scores of Academic Achievement of Adolescent Girls with High, Average and Low Parental Encouragement	47
4.17	Coefficient of Correlation between Parental Encouragement and Academic Achievement of Adolescents	48

LIST OF FIGURES

FIGURE NO.	DESCRIPTIONS	PAGE NO.
4.1	Frequency Polygon of scores of Parental Encouragement of Adolescent Boys and Girls (N = 200)	37
4.2	Frequency Polygon of scores of Parental Encouragement of Adolescents (N = 200)	38
4.3	Frequency Polygon of scores of Academic Achievement of Adolescent Boys and Girls (N = 200)	40
4.4	Frequency Polygon of scores of Academic Achievement of Adolescents (N = 200)	41
4.5	Bar Graph showing Difference of Mean Scores of Parental Encouragement of Adolescent Boys and Girls	42
4.6	Bar Graph showing Difference of Mean Scores of Academic Achievement of Adolescent Boys and Girls	43
4.7	Showing the Mean Scores of Academic Achievement of Adolescents with High, Average and Low Parental Encouragement BOYS	44
4.8	Showing the Mean Scores of Academic Achievement of Adolescent boys with High, Average and Low Parental Encouragement	46
4.9	Showing the Mean Scores of Academic Achievement of Adolescent girls with High, Average and Low Parental Encouragement	47
4.10	Coefficient of Correlation between Parental Encouragement and Academic Achievement of Adolescents	48

CHAPTER – I

INTRODUCTION

"Research is considered to be more formal, systematic intensive process of carrying on the scientific method of analysis. It involves a more systematic structure of investigation, usually resulting in some sort of formal record or procedure and report of results or conclusions."

- *J.W. Best.*

CHAPTER - I
INTRODUCTION

It is a well known fact that education is as old as the human race itself. Since its inception, it has undergone a number of phases and revolutions. It's a never- ending process of inner growth and development which starts right from the conceiving of life till the end of it. In this rapidly changing world of science and technology, the role of education has become vital. It is appropriately regarded as the key to national prosperity and welfare and is the most important form of national investment. Education is the complete development of the individuality of the child, so that he can make an original contribution to human life according to the best of his capability and capacity. Education, in real sense, is to humanize humanity and to make life progressive, cultured and civilized.

Creation of god is so beautiful that we cannot express it in words. It is like the sugar for blind. Parents are the best creation of God. In the lap of parents, children forget all pain and grief of this world. Every child feels protected with his parents. After birth every child moves forward at his path of life with the help of his parents at every step. The blessings of parents are always with their children. Behind every successful person there is always support and help of parents. One can never achieve his/her destination without the guidance of parents. When a person look backward, he/ she realize that it's wholly the parents support and encouragement what he/ she achieves in life. Every great man has the encouragement of parents behind him.

1.1   ADOLESCENCE

Adolescence, no doubt, is the most important period of human life but at the same time it is the most critical period of an individual's development. Adolescence is the phase of development and adjustment, being the traditional period between childhood and adulthood. It is the transitional period in everybody's life, which begins at the end of childhood and closes at the beginning of adulthood. Biologically, adolescence is the age when puberty draws. Chronologically this is a span of life ranging from 12 to 19 years.

The term 'adolescence' comes from the word 'adolescere' which means 'to grow' or 'to grow to maturity'. Maturity not only evolves physical but also mental growth. On the physical side, it means attainment of a mature individual and development of the sex apparatus to make procreation possible. Mentally a mature individual is one whose intelligence has reached its maximum growth. In fact, adolescence period is the time when individuals grow to maturity sexually, intellectually, socially and emotionally. During the phase of adolescence, the individual is neither a child nor a grown up. An adolescent is emotionally unstable during this period. They can't hide their feelings; give expression to their feelings at the right time and in a proper manner. Adolescence is the transitional period from dependence on parents to self-sufficient childhood.

The term adolescence has a broader meaning these days than it had in early years. The adolescent's task is not simply to interact with the external environment or with other individuals but also to develop its own potentialities. They try to expose their role in the world in which they live. It is a stage of new experiences, responsibilities and new relationships with adults as well as peers, which influence his personality, his ability to emerge out of conflicting situations and his futuristic patterns of life.

Psychologically adolescence is a marginal situation, which involves psychological disturbances and problems of adjustment. It differentiates the childhood behavior from adulthood behavior. This period of adolescence, in general, offers an individual a large variety of new experiences and at same time usually finds him less prepared to meet challenges than at any other stage. It has been called a period of stress and strain, storm and strife as all capacities physiological as well as psychological are reaching at a peak.

Harlock (1976) states, "Adolescence is both a way of life and span of time in the physical and psychological development of an individual. It represents a period of growth and change in nearly all aspects of child's physical, mental, social and emotional life. It is the time of new experiences, new responsibilities and new relationships with adults as well as peers."

Collins Cob Wild English Language Dictionary (1991) defines, "Adolescence is the period of one's life in which one develops from being a child into being an adult."

New Illustrated Webster's Dictionary (1992) states, "Adolescence is the process of going up the stage or period of growth from the onset of puberty to the stage to adult development."

According to Oxford English Dictionary (1993), "Adolescence is the process or condition of growing from child to manhood or womanhood, the period of growing up."

According to Chamber's 21st Century Dictionary (1999), "Adolescent is said to be of a young person at the stage of development between adulthood and childhood or between puberty and adulthood."

Dictionary of Psychology (2001) states," Adolescence is a period of development from onset of puberty to attainment of adulthood."

Early adolescence is often marked by changes in school context, family relationships and developmental processes. In the context of these changes, academic performance often declines, while at the same time the long-term implications of academic performance increase. In promoting achievement across elementary and secondary school levels, the significant role of families-family school relations and parental involvement in education has been highlighted.

The scholastic achievement is the most important goal of education. With the achievement in the field of science, education and culture the people have understood the importance of education and have become result oriented. In the process of educating young ones the stress and focus have come to the measurement in school subjects as the teacher grades. Marks obtained are recorded as most valuable guide for classification and placement of students in different occupations at the time of employment. That is why special stress is being given to assessment and examination.

In this rapidly changing world and with growing advancement in science and technology, the place of education has become so vital that every parent today sets high goals to educate his/her child. Parents want the child to shine in academics no matter at what cost! Teacher also sees children's examination performance as measure of their own worth. The test scores, marks or grades assigned to the pupils on the basis of his performance in the achievement tests determine his status with respect to attained skill or knowledge compared with other pupils and also with the adopted standard of the school.

1.2 ACADEMIC ACHIEVEMENT

Modern society is achievement oriented. Academic achievement is the point and center of educational growth and development. It is the most important goal of education. Despite many varied statements about aims of education, the academic achievement of people continues to be the primary and the most important goal of education. Academic achievement creates a challenge for every pupil at all levels of education. It is the status or level of a person's learning and his capability to apply what he has learnt. Academic achievement is the core of a wider term i.e. educational growth, which means growth in all aspects. The assessment of academic achievement has been largely confined to the evaluation in terms of information, knowledge and understanding.

In literal sense, the term 'Academic Achievement' is the combination of two words: Academic + Achievement. It implies 'scholarly accomplishment'. The term 'Academic' has been derived from the term 'Academy' which means a school where special types of instructions are imparted. 'Achievement' means one's learning attainment, accomplishment and proficiency of performance. It refers to the pupil's knowledge attained and skills developed in the school subjects which are assessed by the authorities with the help of achievement tests.

Thus, Academic Achievement in general refers to the degree or level of success or proficiency attained in some specific areas concerning scholastic academic work. Academic achievement plays a significant role in almost all aspects of human life, in shaping the career of an individual and planning for future education. It encourages the students to work hard and learn more. It forms the basis of admission and promotion in a class. Achievement is generally used in the sense of "ability to do, capacity to do or tendency to do" **(Monore and Engelhard, 1952)**. But a person's performance is conditioned by the circumstances, abilities and capacities.

Academic achievement is the achievement related to academic performance. **Good (1974)** defined academic achievement as the knowledge attained or skills developed in the school subjects usually through test scores or there after marks assigned by teacher or both.

According to Crow and Crow (1956), "Academic achievement is the extent to which a learner is profited from instruction in a given area of learning."

According to Dictionary of education (1971), "Academic achievement is the knowledge acquired and skills developed in the school subjects indicated by marks obtained in tests".

According to Kohli (1975), "Academic achievement is the level of proficiency attained in academic work or as finally acquired knowledge in the school subject which is often represented by percentage of marks obtained by students in an examination"

According to Wolman (1976), "Academic achievement is the degree or level of proficiency attained in scholastic or academic work."

According to Christian (1980), "The word achievement indicates the learning outcomes of the students. As a result of learning different subjects, the behaviour pattern of students changes".

Stephen (1980) stated that academic achievement is the unique responsibility of educational institution established by the society to promote the wholesome scholastic development of the pupil."

According to Sullivan (1987), "Academic achievement is the level of learning in a partitioned area of subjects in terms of knowledge, understanding, skill and application; usually designed by test scores or marks assigned by the teacher or both."

According to Taneja's Dictionary of Education (1988), "Academic achievement represents intellectual growth and the ability to participate in the production of knowledge. At its worst achievement represents inculcation of mindless indoctrination of the young."

According to new Webster's Dictionary (1990), "Academic achievement is the performance of student in a course based on format studied in an institution of learning."

Torres (1994) defined academic achievement as. "The attained ability or degree of competence in school tasks usually measured by standardized test and expressed in grades or units based on norms, derived from a wide sampling of pupil's performance."

Random House Webster's College Thesaurus (1997) stated that academic achievement means those qualities or attributes or characteristics or traits of an individual which contribute to or have a direct bearing or effect or influence on the accomplishment or proficiency of performance, pertaining to any activity, scholastic in nature or any scholarly activity.

According to Ladson (1999), "At its best Academic Achievement represents intellectual growth and ability to participate in the production of knowledge. At its worst, academic achievement represents inculcation and mindless indoctrination of the young into the cannons and orthodoxy of the old."

According to Oxford Advanced Learner's Dictionary (2000), "Achievement is the thing that somebody has done successfully, especially using his/her effort and skill."

Kumari (2001) defined academic achievement as the sum total of information gained after completing a course of instruction particularly or fully in a particular grade that he has obtained on an achievement test."

According to Merriam Webster's Collegiate Dictionary (2001), "Achievement is an art of achieving a result gained by efforts; the quality and quantity of students work."

According to Ollendik (2003), "Academic Achievement is defined as the knowledge and skills that an individual learns through direct instruction. Achievement tests measure what a person has learned, where an aptitude test (including that of intelligence) assess a person's potential for learning."

According To Subramanyam (2008), "Education achievement is usually defined in three ways; the grades the students earn in school, their performance and standardized tests of academic achievement or the number of years of schooling completed."

Academic achievement is the accomplishment or proficiency of performance in a given skill or body of knowledge. It means the amount of knowledge gained by the student in different subjects of study. Academic achievement is the act of achieving or furnishing something that has been attained successfully especially by means of skills, perseverance or practice. Academic achievement is related to the acquisition of principles, generalizations and the capacity to perform efficiently (certain manipulations of objects, symbols and ideas). Assessment of academic performance has been largely confirmed to the evaluation in terms of information, knowledge and understanding. It is universally accepted that the acquisition of factual data is not an end in itself but an individual who has received education should show evidence of having understood them. For obvious reason the examinations are largely confined to the measurement of the amount of information which students have acquired. It is perhaps the only expected basis for promotion or to fulfill the requirement for any degree or diploma. It is the actual or assumed possession of knowledge that counts either for admission into a class or course.

Academic achievement has a very high place in child's life. It builds self-esteem and provides self-confidence and above all, emotional security. Academic achievements have come to occupy the central position. Sound development in academic record is just like the pillars on which entire future structure of personality stand. Academic achievement is related to the acquisition of principles and generalizations and the capacity to perform efficiently certain manipulations of objects, symbols and ideas. Thus, academic achievement is

a) Quantity and quality of learning attained in a subject or a group of subjects after a period of instruction.
b) Knowledge attained or skills developed in school subjects.

Thus, academic achievement has become an index of a child's future in this highly competitive world. It is only a drop in the vast sea of education. Academic achievement or Scholastic Achievement means the attained level at which the student is functioning in school such as Economics, History and English as measured by the school marks. Thus, academic achievement of a pupil refers to the knowledge attained and skills developed in school subjects, which are assessed by educational authorities with the help of achievement test which may be standardized or non-standardized.

It is found that there are number of factors which may be considered responsible for high and low achievement of the students. Thus it will be of immense interest and importance for a researcher to know these factors which are contributing to the academic achievement. Broadly, these factors may be categorized under the two headings:-

(I) Subjective factors
(II) Objective factors

(I) Subjective Factors

These are factors pertaining to self of the individual. They include
(a) Study habits
(b) Interest
(c) Motivation
(d) Level of Aspiration
(e) Intelligence
(f) Attitude towards course
(g) Self Esteem
(h) Socio-economic status
(i) Aptitude
(j) Creativity

(II) Objective Factors

The objective factors include:
(a) Personal Background
(b) Teaching Method
(c) Examination System
(d) Medium of instruction
(e) Educational faculties

These factors affect the academic achievement both positively as well as adversely. These are the various aspects of the concept of academic achievement, which has a great bearing on the personality of the student. On early age, sense of achievement is a source of good feeling & self esteem and failure is a source of anger & self-reproach. So students need to perform themselves not only to work hard to achieve their academic goals but also to cope with the multitude of stresses in the personal social, academic and vocational domains endemic to the school context. In the present scenario academic achievement is the concern of parents, teachers and students.

School achievement may be affected by different factors like study habits, intelligence and attitudes of learners towards school, socio economic status and different aspects of their personality etc. In our society academic achievement is considered as a key principle to judge one's total capacities and potentialities. Hence academic achievement possesses a very imperative place in education as well as in the learning process. As Crow and Crow, 1969 defined Academic achievement as the extent to which a learner is profiting from instructions in the given area of learning i.e. achievement is reflected by the level to which skill and knowledge has been imparted to him. Academic achievement also indicates the knowledge attained and skill developed in the school subject, generally designated by test scores. Achievement is influenced by the personality, opportunities, motivation, training and education. The other factors which influence the academic achievement of student are self-concept, study habit, parental encouragement, socio economic status, intelligence etc.

1.3 PARENTAL ENCOURAGEMENT

Parental encouragement is important in shaping attitude, values, self confidence and behavior of child. It refers to the treatment originating from parents towards the child with a view to enhance the possibilities, if future occurrences of good behavior by care, concern, approval and guidance.

Parental Encouragement is one of the aspects of parent's treatment patterns. The parents help the child, guide him and coax him so that he may not feel disheartened at a particular point of difficulty. The entire treatment may have many individual traits. But contents and directions are the same i.e. to give encouragement to the child. It may be in form of approval or may be in the form of asking the child to modify his behavior in the child which amounts to discouragements. Parental encouragement, as a term in education, has very explicitly has been defined by *Rossi* in these words:

> *"When father and mother approve or appreciate any activity related to education or revoke any hurdle felt by the student in the process, or guide him the right and wrong - this entire spectrum activity comes within the purview of "Parental Encouragement".*

According to Chaube (1983) "If the individual is not having proper parental encouragement, he may develop complexes. This makes him mal- adjusted in life in various ways. The parental encouragement is not only important for individual development but for the future life also. Thus parental encouragement is the backbone of the adolescent's personal life."

According to Sharma (1988), "Parental Encouragement is the treatment of originating from parents towards the child with a view to enhance the possibilities of the future occurrence of good behavior by care, concern, approval and guidance."

According to Thomson (1989) "Mother has more opportunity than the father to influence her child's psychological group and behavior. Tradition also favors' the mother's influence since child rearing in our culture is generally recognized as primarily mother's privilege and responsibility.'

Oxford Advanced Learner Dictionary(1989) states, "Parental Encouragement is referred to ones father or mother encouragement means is given to support confidence or hope, to encouragement means action of encouraging shows of encouragement thing that encourages."

According to Grolnick and slowiaczek(1994) defined that parental involvement as the allocation of resources to the child's academic endeavor.

The family is the oldest, basic and fundamental unit of human society. It consists of the husband, wife, children together with all the young and all dependents. They are related to one another is one way or the other. Thus family may be regarded as a small social group consisting of a few related persons. In our country, in family parents are considered as God. God is the supreme power in the world. Parents are the best creation of the creator, every child feels protected in lap of his parents. After his birth every child moves forward at his path of life and gets help of his parents at every step. He always finds their blessings, hands on his head. Every successful person after reaching his destination finds that his success is because of the help of his bringing up finds that these were his parents who has been performing a great role to make the life a success. They shine like sun on the sky of this world. Every great man and child has encouragement of their parents behind their success. Soldiers, who are fighting at the border and destroy the troops of enemies of their country, they say, destroy! The enemies of your mother India always raise high." Thus children have the encouragement of their parents behind them.

From the time of birth, child's personality is molded by the family in which he lives. If the child finds a healthy environment at home he has all chances for development of all round personality. It is not the number of family members which is being observed in many cases. Present families are able to inculcate many values in their members. Even two individuals of the same family do not get same home environment& encouragement.

The parents seem to play a very important role in molding their children character, personality, career and advancement in education. They may differently devote their attention, time and efforts to different domains such as child's social, religious activities, academics and athletics i.e. traditional phase of growth and development between childhood and adulthood.

The term "Parental Encouragement" refers to the treatment originating from parents towards the child with a view to enhance the possibilities if future occurrences of good behavior by care, concern, approval and guidance. Parental Encouragement is one of the aspects of parent treatment patterns. The parents help the child, guide him and coax him so that he may not feel disheartened at a particular point of difficulty. The entire treatment may have many individual traits. But their contents and directions are the same .i.e. to give encouragement to the child. It may be in the form of approval or may be in the form of asking in the child to modify his behavior. In case, it creates avoidance behavior in the child which amounts to discouragement. Parental Encouragement is of great significance in developing psychological as well as academic behavior of a child. There are many factors which affect the Parental Encouragement:

1.3.1 FACTORS AFFECTING PARENTAL ENCOURAGEMENT

1. **Social status of the parents:** If the social status of the parents is high in the society, their parental encouragement will also high because they want their children should also get high position in the society. But the parents who have low social status, their Parental Encouragement will be low.
2. **Economic status of the parents:** Economic status is related to income of parents. Economic status of the parents also affects the Parental Encouragement. Parents whose economic status is low, also has low Parental Encouragement. In some cases, it may be high but they lack economic sources.
3. **Psychological status:** Psychological status is concerned to the emotions feelings, anger, thirst, ideas etc. parents who are of open minded and think that education is necessary for child, development of child is essential for better life and time should be given to child for his development, they have high Parental Encouragement. But the parent's orthodox attitude who thinks that education is not necessary for the life. Children should do work with them have low Parental Encouragement.
4. **Educational status of the parents:** Educational status is concerned with general, technical of professional education of the person. Educational status of the parents also affects the Parental Encouragement of the child. Parents of high education level will have high Parental Encouragement because they know the importance of the education. But the parents with low educational level will provide low Parental Encouragement because they do not know the importance of education in life.
5. **Effect of urban and rural area:** Urban children will have high Parental Encouragement because they have basic facilities for their proper development. Rural children have low Parental Encouragement because the lack of facilities. But in some cases it may be high because today farmer families also want to give education to their children and providing facilities for their development.
6. **Effect of home environment:** Family plays an important role of the educational and vocational progress of the children. Three types of parental attitudes: acceptance, concentration, and avoidance are also associated with the educational and vocational development of the students. Attitudes which parents express towards their sons and daughters develop certain attitudes towards the home environment. That formation of attitude in the early stages of life plays a very significant role in the development process of individual's behavior. Parental acceptance plays major role in determining the attitude and behavior of the person.

1.4 STATEMENT OF THE STUDY
A STUDY OF ACADEMIC ACHIEVEMENT OF ADOLESCENTS IN RELATION TO PARENTAL ENCOURAGEMENT

1.5 OPERATIONAL DEFINITIONS
ACADEMIC ACHIEVEMENT

Academic Achievement refers to the pupil's knowledge attained and skills developed in the school subjects which are assessed by the authorities with the help of achievement tests. Academic Achievement in general refers to the degree or level of success or proficiency attained in some specific areas concerning scholastic academic work.

PARENTAL ENCOURAGEMENT

Parental Encouragement refers to the treatment originating from parents towards the child with a view to enhance the possibilities of future occurrences of good behavior by care, concern, approval and guidance.

1.6 OBJECTIVES OF STUDY

The following are the objectives laid down for the present study:
1. To study and compare parental encouragement of adolescent boys and girls.
2. To study and compare academic achievement of adolescent boys and girls.
3. To study the relationship between parental encouragement and academic achievement of adolescent boys and girls.

1.7 SIGNIFICANCE OF THE STUDY

Children are the most important asset of a country. It is they who will become tomorrow's young men and will provide the human potential required for the country's development. It is therefore necessary that today's child should be healthy both physically and mentally so that tomorrow he may prove to be an energetic and dynamic young man. School education is an important segment of the total educational system contributing significantly to the individual as well as to national development. A good school provides environment conducive for development of cognitive, affective and psychomotor domains for all round development of individual.

An achievement test is a measure of an individual's degree of accomplishment or learning in a subject or task. The achievement test serves as a tool to measure current knowledge levels for the purpose of placing students in an educational environment where they have the chance to advance at a pace that is suitable for their abilities. The assessment of academic achievement also provides feedback both to teachers and parents. It helps the teachers to know whether the teaching methods are effective or not and helps them in bringing improvement accordingly. In the world today, where knowledge is being multiplied exponentially, education is not justifying itself by remaining merely contented with the objective of imparting of certain amount of knowledge but should help to improve the quality of life. One is to acquire knowledge; other is to acquire the ability the ability to use knowledge. Life is becoming complex day by day. In the present scenario youth as well as children are facing difficulties. It has been observed that the families and communities are important in helping youth develop their knowledge and skills, to make them emotionally mature so that they can obtain technologically sophisticated jobs which are emerging part of the society.

Academic achievement plays an important role in the life of the child and helps to elevate the social economics status of individual as well as family. Parental Encouragement plays a supporting role in habit formation & personality development of an individual specifically in case of adolescence. It is the stage where maximum growth and development of adolescence take place.

Today, adolescents live in a society which has become multi-complex, thus making the roles of adolescents very diffuse and confusing. The roles of adolescents and their development, as tasks are no longer well defined and prescribed. Knowledge explosion, material wealth pursuit, plurality of society and estrangement from the extended family system, the hypocrisy of adult standards and the fallacy of physical maturity all present a great battle for adolescents to fight with the dilemma of indefinite status. They are facing problems like peer pressure and competition, adjustments at home and society, in general making them frustrated which affect their academic achievement. Good academic achievement of adolescents directly related or depends upon parental encouragement. Thus, investigator attempts to study how academic achievement of adolescents is affected by parental encouragement.

1.8 DELIMITATIONS OF THE STUDY
1. The study is confined to adolescents of District Hoshiarpur .
2. The study is conducted on 200 adolescents (100 girls and 100 boys).
3. Study is delimited to class 9th students only.

1.9 STATISTICAL TECHNIQUES USED
1. Descriptive statistical techniques like mean and standard deviation.
2. Correlation is used to find out the relationship
3. t- Test is employed to check the significance of difference between means.

CHAPTER – II

REVIEW OF RELATED LITERATURE

"Practically all human knowledge can be found in books and libraries unlike other animals that start a new with each generation, man builds upon the accumulated and recorded knowledge of the past"

- *J.W. Best.*

CHAPTER - II
REVIEW OF RELATED LITERATURE

Man is the only social animal who can take advantage of knowledge which has been preserved and accumulated through the centuries or since the origin of man. Human knowledge has three phases- preservation, transmission and advancement. This fact is of particular importance in research which operates as continues function of ever closer approximate to the truth. Practically all human knowledge can be found in books and libraries. Unlike all other animals that might start a new with each generation man builds upon the accumulated and recorded knowledge of the past. His constant adding to the vast store of the knowledge makes possible progress in all areas of human endeavor. Similarly for any specific research project to occupy this place in the development of discipline the researcher must be thoroughly familiar with both previous research and theory.

Any worthwhile research study in any field of knowledge requires an adequate familiarity with the work which has already been done in the same area. It can never be undertaken in isolation of the work that has already been done on the problems which are directly or indirectly related to a study proposed by a researcher. A summary of the writings of recognized authorities and of previous research provides evidence that the researcher is familiar with what is already known and what is still unknown and untested. Since effective research is based upon past knowledge, this step helps to eliminate the duplication of what has been done and provides useful hypotheses and helpful.

MEANING OF REVIEW OF RELATED LITERATURE

The phrase 'review of related literature' consists of two words Review and Literature, where 'review' means 'to organize the knowledge of the specific area of research and to show that the proposed study would be an addition to this field in research methodology'. 'Literature' means knowledge of a particular area of investigation of and discipline which includes theoretical and practical area, in other words, literature stands for a collective body of related works done in the post by earlier researchers. The literature consists of the published and unpublished research that are relevant to your own research question will likely includes articles in journals, books or chapters inedited books, conference papers, documents published on the web. According to Monly, "Literature is the mirror which reflects the post views and presents the future prospective. To develop an insight into and gives a guideline to investigator. Review of relate the literature is an essentially aspect of investigation."

Survey of related research means a careful perusal of researches already done and writes ups published or lecture delivered on issues directly or indirectly connected with the problem being proposed for investigation. It means having a soaking into the waters of knowledge which has relevance to the study in hand.

Every research begins from where the previous researchers have lift in and goes forward, may be one inch or even less towards the solution of the problem or answer of the question. Therefore for ever researcher it is essential to acquaint himself with what already has been thought, expressed and done about the problem under investigation. This is possible only if he/she reviews and surveys books, journals, newspapers, records, documents, thesis, abstracts, dissertations and other sources of information directly or indirectly concerned with the problem of investigation. The study of related literature implies locating, reading and evaluating reports of research as well as reports of casual information and opinions are related to the individual's planned research project.

Research takes advantages of the knowledge which has accumulated in the past as a result of constant human endeavor. A careful review of the research journal, books, dissertations these and other sources of information on the problem to be investigated is one of the important steps in the planning of any research study. Citing studies that show substantial agreement and those that seem to present conflicting conclusion helps to sharpen and define understanding of existing knowledge in the problem area, provides a background for the research project and makes the investigator aware about the status of the issue. The review of related literature is an appraising description of information found in the literature associated to the chosen area of research. It gives a hypothetical foundation for the research and helps to establish the nature of research. It plays an important role while pursuing any research because of the following reasons:

1. The review of related literature enables the researcher to define the limits of his field. It helps the researcher to delimit and define the problem. The knowledge of research literature, brings the researcher up-to-date on the work which others have done and thus to state the objective clearly and concisely.
2. The researcher can avoid unfruitful and useless problem areas. He can select those areas in which positive findings are very likely to result and his endeavors in which positive findings are very likely to result and his endeavors would be likely to add to the knowledge in a meaningful way.
3. It helps the researcher to avoid unintentional duplication of well established findings. The review of related literature gives the researcher an understanding of the research methodology which refers to the way the study is to be conducted.
4. It helps the researcher to know about the tools and instruments which proved to be useful and promising in the previous studies. It also provides insight into the statistical methods through which validity of results is to be established.
5. The final and important specific reason for reviewing the related literature is to know about the recommendations of the previous researchers listed in their studies for further research.

Thus, the review of related literature helps the investigator in identifying the theories that need further exploration in developing a perspective to ascertain the general trends in the area in locating the problem, yet unexplored in selecting the appropriate methodology of research. The present chapter is a humble attempt to refer to the most relevant studies and material which the investigator happened to go through while searching for related literature.

2.1 STUDIES RELATED TO ACADEMIC ACHIEVEMENT

Wentzel (1991) conducted a study on relations between social competence and academic achievement in early adolescence. Relations between academic performance and 3 aspects of social competence—socially responsible behavior, sociometric status, and self-regulatory processes (goal setting, interpersonal trust, and problem-solving styles) were studied. Correlational findings indicate that each aspect of social competence is related significantly to students' grades. Results from multiple regression analyses suggest that when accounting for students' IQ, sex, ethnicity, school absence, and family structure, socially responsible behavior mediates almost entirely the relations between students' grades and the other 2 aspects of social competence. Socailly responsible behaviour and peer status appear to be related by way of their joint association with goals to be socially responsible, interpersonal trust, and problem- solving styles.

Norman (1995) conducted a study on predicting antisocial behavior in youngsters displaying poor academic achievement: A review of risk factors. It was indicated that school failure tends to be associated with other negative behaviors, and that delinquency has been found to be a common co-occurring difficulty. Factors thought to contribute to the co-occurrence of school failure and delinquency was discussed with the goal of helping clinicians identify among youngsters failing at school-those most likely to develop antisocial behavior. The factors addressed include temperament, intelligence, school attitude, peer influence, and parenting practices. The implications of these risk factors for early assessment and treatment were discussed.

Sander (1996) carried out a study entitled, "Catholic grade schools and academic achievement".In this study the effect of a Catholic grade school education on the test scores of non-Hispanic whites is examined. Particular attention is given to the issue of selection into the Catholic grade school sector. It is shown that eight years in a Catholic grade school is associated with higher vocabulary, mathematics, and reading test scores. No Catholic grade school effect is found on science test scores. Further, it is shown that there is not positive selection into the Catholic school sector. Thus, higher test scores cannot be attributed to selecting superior students. It is also shown that the positive Catholic schooling effect is driven by non-Catholics who attend Catholic grade schools. Once non-Catholic in Catholic schools are eliminated from the sample, the Catholic school effect becomes zero.

Sanders and Rivers (1996) in their study on Cumulative and residual effects of teachers on future student academic achievement showed that differences in student achievement of 50 percentile points were observed as a result of teacher sequence after only three years. The effects of teachers on student achievement are both additive and cumulative with little evidence of compensatory effects. As teacher effectiveness increases, lower achieving students are the first to benefit. The top quintile of teachers facilitate appropriate to excellent gains for students of all achievement levels. Students of different ethnicities respond equivalently within the same quintile of teacher effectiveness.

Agrawal and Pande (1997) designed a study on influence of parental encouragement on educational achievement of students. The results showed that the high achieving students got the highest amount of parental encouragement. However, the middel group of students got lesser amount of parental encouragement than those of lower group.

Marsh and Yeung (1997) conducted a study on causal effects of academic self-concept on academic achievement: Structural equation models of longitudinal data. Academic self-concept, school marks, and teacher ratings of achievement were collected in 3 high-school subjects in each of 3 years (N=603). In the structural equation models (SEMs) considered, both school-based performance and academic self-concept were measured with multiple indicators for each school subject. SEMs were used to evaluate the effects of prior academic self-concept on subsequent achievement after controlling for the effects of prior achievement, and the effects of prior achievement on subsequent academic self-concept after controlling for the effects of prior academic self-concept. Although the effects of achievement tended to be larger and more systematic, there was clear support for both academic self-concept and achievement effects. Although there was support for this reciprocal effects model for all 3 school subjects, self-concept effects tended to be larger and more systematic for mathematics than for science and, particularly, English.

Jain and Mishra (1998) conducted a study on impact of socialization on academic achievement: study of adolescents. Regression analysis revealed that the parental responsiveness was the only factor which significantly and positively contributed to academic achievement.

Verma and Sheikh (1998) presented a study on personality traits and needs as correlates of academic achievement. The findings of the study lead to the conclusion that not all, but some personality traits and personality needs contribute towards scholastic achievement of adolescent girls.

Fan and Chen (2001) in their study entitled, "Parental involvement and students' academic achievement: A meta-analysis" revealed a small to moderate, and practically meaningful, relationship between parental involvement and academic achievement. Through moderator analysis, it was revealed that parental aspiration/expectation for children's education achievement has the strongest relationship, whereas parental home supervision has the weakest relationship, with students' academic achievement. In addition the relationship is stronger when academic achievement is represented by a global indicator (e.g. GPA) than by a subject specific indicator (e.g. math grade).

Sharma and Renu (2003) conducted a study on effect of social inquiry model on pupil's achievement in social science. Analysis of results revealed that students taught by Social Inquiry Model exhibited superior performance as compared to their counterparts taught by conventional classroom teaching.

Kasinath (2003) in his study on piagetian conservation abilities as determinants of academic achievement investigated the effect of selected piagetian conservation ability on academic achievement in science. A significant positive relationship was observed between academic achievement and selected piagetian conservation ability.

Valentine et al. (2004) conducted a study on the relation between self-beliefs and academic achievement: A meta-analytic review. There has been extensive debate among scholars and practitioners concerning whether self-beliefs influence academic achievement. To address this question, findings of longitudinal studies investigating the relation between self-beliefs and achievement were synthesized using meta-analysis. Estimated effects are consistent with a small, favorable influence of positive self-beliefs on academic achievement, with an average standardized path or regression coefficient of .08 for self-beliefs as a predictor of later achievement, controlling for initial levels of achievement. Stronger effects of self-beliefs are evident when assessing self-beliefs specific to the academic domain and when measures of self-beliefs and achievement are matched by domain (e.g., same subject area).

Rivkin et al. (2005) conducted a study on teachers, schools, and academic achievement. This paper disentangles the impact of schools and teachers in influencing achievement with special attention given to the potential problems of omitted or mismeasured variables and of student and school selection. Unique matched panel data from the UTD Texas Schools Project permit the identification of teacher quality based on student performance along with the impact of specific, measured components of teachers and schools. Semi- parametric lower bound estimates of the variance in teacher quality based entirely on within-school heterogeneity indicate that teachers have powerful effects on reading and mathematics achievement, though little of the variation in teacher quality is explained by observable characteristics such as education or experience. The results suggest that the effects of a costly ten student reduction in class size are smaller than the benefit of moving one standard deviation up the teacher quality distribution, highlighting the importance of teacher effectiveness in the determination of school quality.

Sirin (2005) in his study on socioeconomic status and academic achievement: A meta-analytic review of research showed a medium to strong SES–achievement relation. This relation, however, is moderated by the unit, the source, the range of SES variable, and the type of SES–achievement measure. The relation is also contingent upon school level, minority status, and school location. The author conducted a replica of White's (1982) meta-analysis to see whether the SES–achievement correlation had changed since White's initial review was published. The results showed a slight decrease in the average correlation.

Bajwa and Kaur, (2006) studied " Academic achievement in relation to family environment and academic stress" and concluded that there exists a significant relationship between academic achievement and competitive framework, dimensions of family environment, significant relation between academic achievement and dimension of the family environment.

Alim and Naseem (2008) designed a study on mother's working status and academic achievement of adolescents. Results of the study revealed that there was a significant difference in academic achievement of children of working and non-working mothers. Significant difference in academic achievement of boys and girls of working mothers was also found. There were significant differences in academic achievement of boys and girls of non-working mothers. Academic achievement of boys of working and non-working mothers also showed same trends. Likeness to mother was highest in girl's group of working mothers. Democratic parenting has been found practiced highest in girls' group of working mothers. Willingness to stay at home at free time was found to be highest amongst girls' group of working mothers.

Lodi & Tyagi (2008) conducted a study on exploration of the impact of social intelligence on academic achievement. The findings of the study lead to the conclusion that the social intelligence scores are normally distributed in the universe. The students of different faculties differ in their social intelligence. Commerce students have the highest social intelligence scores and the Arts students have the lowest while the science students are between the two. Among the three disciplines commerce students require the highest level of social intelligence, science the middle and arts the lowest. Social intelligence has a significant correlation in determining academic achievement of science girls, commerce girls and arts boys & girls. But it is insignificant in case of science boys and total science students, commerce boys and total commerce students, total arts students and total students of all the faculties.

Mohalik (2008) designed a study on impact of in-service teacher education programmes on teacher effectiveness and students' achievement in English. The study concluded that teacher effectiveness of secondary school English teachers was related to their participation in in-service teacher education programmes and students' achievement in English is also influenced by teachers' participation in such programmes.

Singh (2008) conducted a study to find out the relationship between learning style preferences and academic achievement of high school pupils. The findings of the study were :(a) flexible, aural, short-attention span, non-motivation centered, learning styles (preferences) had been observed to be positively affecting the academic achievement of urban-pupils (both boys & girls), (b) non-flexible, visual, non-motivation centered and environment free learning styles (preferences) had been observed to be positively affecting the academic achievement of rural pupils (both boys & and girls).

Kumar et al. (2009) in their study entitled, "Study habits and academic achievement of the students at secondary". The result indicates that students with different academic achievement differ significantly on their study habits. It is also clear that high achieving students had significantly superior study habits than average achieving students and low achieving students. Similarly average achieving students had significantly superior study habits than low achieving students.

Minakshi (2009) conducted a study on the study of human values on academic achievement and gender of teacher trainees. The study revealed that the boys have demonstrated favorable attitude than girls towards value education categorized on the basis of different levels of their academic achievement. Attitude of the participants towards value education categorized on the basis of different levels of their academic achievement differs significantly to each other. It is clearly revealed that the academic achievement is found to have significant impact on the attitude towards value education. Academic achievement and gender influence significant the attitude towards value education of the participants.

Sunder (2009) conducted a study on academic achievement and intelligence of students of bachelor of education. The study revealed that there is no significant difference between the mean score of academic achievement of boys and girls students of Bachelor of Education. Girls students were found to be better than boys on both dimensions.

Augustine (2010) carried out a study to understand the extent of relationship between teaching aptitude, teaching competency, academic background and achievement in educational psychology of student-teachers in the colleges of education. The study revealed the following: (i) There is no consistent positive relationship between academic background and teaching aptitude of student teachers. (ii) There is no significant positive relationship between teaching aptitude and achievement in educational psychology.

Chaudhari (2010) carried out a study entitled, "The Academic Achievement of Tribal Students of Ashram School of Surat District". The findings of the study revealed that the academic achievement of tribal students of Ashram schools of Surat district was found average in Gujarati, Hindi, Social Science and Mathematics, while below average in English and Science & Technology. So there was a need to find out the reason behind their different levels of achievement in different subjects.

Dakshinamurthy (2010) designed a study on effect of teacher's personality, attitude towards profession and teaching effectiveness on academic achievement of students. The results indicated that in the total sample there is impact of teacher's personality, attitude towards profession and their teaching effectiveness on academic achievement of the students. But in 2-way interaction there is no significant relationship found between teachers' personality and teaching effectiveness on academic achievement of students and teachers' attitude towards profession and teaching effectiveness on academic achievement of students. In 3-way interaction there is a positive relationship between teachers' personality, attitude towards profession and teaching effectiveness of secondary school teachers on academic achievement of students.

Mathur and Baghel (2010) conducted a study to assess the effect of sleep deprivation on health and academic achievement of adolescents. The results revealed that the effect of sleep deprivation on health and academic achievement among male and female students of Science and Arts steams was highly affected by sleep deprivation. The results also revealed that relationship of sleep deprivation with health problem is positive but with academic achievement it is negative.

Pany (2010) designed a study on effect of making of familiar strange MFS approach of synectics model of teaching on creativity, academic achievement and achievement motivation of learners. The analysis of the obtained data revealed that (i) the MFS approach of synectics model of teaching is the effective one in enhancing the creative thinking ability of the learner (ii) the MFS approach of synectics is not useful in enhancing the achievement motivation of the learners, and (iii) the MFS approach of synectics is not useful in enhancing the academic achievement of the learners in subjects like General Science, Geography and English.

Vasanthi (2010) in his study on learning environment and academic achievement of higher secondary physics students found that the correlation between learning environment and academic achievement, and learning environment and socioeconomic status vary significantly.

Asthana (2011) deigned a study on self-concept, mental ability and scholastic achievement of secondary school students of Varanasi. Findings of the study revealed that there was a significant difference in male and female students regarding their scholastic achievement. Girls were better than boys in academic performance. Mental ability and self-concept were positively and significantly related to scholastic achievement. Moderated regression analysis as well as subgroup analysis revealed that relationship between mental ability and scholastic achievement is moderated by self-concept.

Basu and Agnihotri (2011) carried out a study entitled, "Emotional stability of adolescents in relation to their academic achievement". The results of the study indicate that while male and female adolescents do not differ significantly in their levels of emotional stability, students from Hindi and English medium schools differ in a significant manner. Also a significant relationship is found between emotional stability and academic achievement of the adolescents.

Devaki and Pushpam (2011) conducted a study on metacognitive ability academic achievement in Chemistry. They found that there is significant association between metacognitive ability and academic achievement in Chemistry.

Farzana (2011) conducted a study on impact of birth order on academic achievement of high school students. He found that birth order does not have significant impact on the performance of students.

Harish (2011) conducted an investigation on impact of integrated critical thinking skills on achievement in mathematics of secondary school students. The study revealed that the package of integrated critical thinking skills has a significant impact on the academic achievement of standard 9 students in mathematics. The study also revealed that the boys and girls do not differ in their achievement in mathematics. However, group and gender have their significant interaction effect on achievement in mathematics.

Hemamalini (2011) in her study on anxiety and academic achievement of high school students of Mysore city found a significant negative relationship between anxiety and academic achievement of high school students. The study revealed that both very high and very low anxiety levels lead to low academic achievement among the high school students.

Kapil and Gupta (2011) in their study on stress management techniques and academic performance among adolescents showed that girls preferred social support technique more as compared to positive attitude for improving their academic performance, whereas boys preferred positive attitude technique more than social support technique.

Kaur and Sharma (2011) in their study on effect of Abacus technique on achievement in mathematics at elementary stage found that there is significant difference in the achievement of experimental group (taught with abacus) and controlled group (taught without abacus). They concluded that teaching the 5th grade students using abacus is beneficial for the students in improving their achievement in mathematics. The achievement scores of boys and girls of different schools of experimental group showed that gender has no significant effect on the mathematics achievement of students. Further, the achievement scores of students of experimental group with different levels of intelligence i.e. high, average and low have significant difference.

Kaur and Singh (2011) in their study entitled, "Study of academic achievement in relation to emotional intelligence of adolescents" revealed that there is positive and significant relationship between academic achievement and emotional intelligence. On the basis of these results it is suggested that the parents and the teachers should help in the development of emotional intelligence, create conducive environment for the development of emotional maturity among the adolescents. This will help in the improvement of academic achievement of the students.

Pannu and Singh (2011) conducted a study on influence of adjustment on academic achievement of adolescent students. Results of ANOVA showed that home, health and emotional adjustment influence the academic achievement of adolescents but social adjustment influenced the academic achievements of adolescents but social adjustment did not influence the academic achievement of adolescents.

Raju and Samiullah (2011) attempted to study the impact of parental involvement on academic achievement of XII standard students. The results revealed that students with high parental involvement had shown better academic achievement as compared to students low parental involvement. There was no significant difference in the academic achievement of the students studying in government and private schools.

Sadanandan and Lourdusamy (2011) conducted a study entitled, "Parental Influence on Academic Achievement of Higher Secondary Students". The investigators found a significant relationship between scholastic performance of students and parental influence though there was no significant relationship between scholastic performance of students and their parenting, family and school relationship.

Sharma and Khatoon (2011) carried out a study entitled "Family Variables as Predictors of Students' Achievement in Science". The results indicated that parental education, parental occupation and family size contributed significantly to science achievement of the students. But no difference in science achievement was found between children whose fathers were either in the professional or in businessmen group.

Sharma and Sharma (2011) designed a study on relationship of academic achievement of students with thinking styles. A significant relationship between judicial thinking style and academic achievement was observed. Moreover, females were found to be disposed more towards the use of executive and judicial thinking style than their counterpart males. Also the students of arts stream had greater preference towards the use of executive and judicial thinking style than the students of science stream.

Shelly (2011) attempted to examine the relationship among personality traits, approaches to learning, study skills and academic achievement of Pharmacy students. The findings of the study indicated that intellect trait predicted the deep learning approach; the conscientiousness trait predicted the strategic learning approach; and the emotional stability trait negatively predicted the surface learning approach. As expected, both deep learning approach and strategic learning approach were positively associated with academic performance where as the surface learning approach negatively predicted achievement.

Singh (2011) carried out a study entitled, "Study habits in relation to anxiety and achievement". The results indicated that high and average anxiety groups show significant difference in their mean scores of study habits. Therefore, it can be concluded that average anxiety group has better study habits than high and very low anxiety level. Not only these, those students who have average anxiety show better academic performance than other two types because they bear regular study habits.

Sharma, S. and Priya (2011) studied the difference in academic performance and academic anxiety of rural adolescents. This investigation was conducted to study the difference in academic performance of adolescents at various levels of academic anxiety. A total sample of 200 (100 boys and 100 girls) adolescents in the age range of 13-16 years, from different high and senior secondary schools of Ludhiana district were purposely selected. Based on their performance, the sample was divided into two groups, vis high performance (>70% marks) and low performers (<45%marks). Socio economic status scale (2001) was used to judge the socio economic status of the respondents. To measure the level of perceived parental encouragement scale (1999) and academic anxiety scale for children (1984) were used. The result indicated that academic performance of adolescent boys was not significantly different across various levels of academic anxiety. Further significant difference was found between low and high performing adolescent girls at various levels of academic anxiety.

Fatima et al. (2012) conducted a study on impact of achievement goals, sociability and gender on academic achievement of university students. Regression analysis showed that only performance-approach goals significantly predicted academic achievement. Independent sample t-test demonstrated that girls are significantly high on academic achievement and performance-approach goals whereas boys were significantly more sociable.

Singh and Thukral (2011) conducted a study on emotional maturity and academic achievement of high school students. The study was designed to investigate the relationship of emotional maturity with academic achievement of high school students and also to see the sex and regional differences on the basis of their emotional maturity. The results revealed that there exists no significant relationship between emotional maturity and academic achievement. No significant differences were observed between boys and girls as well as rural and urban students on the basis of their emotional maturity.

Sutherman and Vasanthi (2011) designed a study on study habits and academic achievement of XI standard students in Palani educational district. From the study it was observed that the mean scores of girls' study habits and their academic achievement are more than boys. This may be due to the hard work and sincerity of girls when compared to boys.

Tiwari and Naithani (2011) designed a study on impact of parent child relationship on scholastic achievement of adolescents. Findings of the study revealed that children of highly protective parents score less marks in all the subjects. Children of loving parents scored higher in all the four subjects than the children of parents who scored low on loving dimension. It was also found that parents who are not very demanding, their children scored higher in three subjects than the children of highly demanding parents.

Kaur (2013) investigated to find out the relationship between academic achievement and emotional intelligence. The results of the study revealed a positive and significant difference between academic achievement of adolescent boys and girls. The mean scores of adolescent boys were higher than that of adolescent girls on academic achievement, concluding that adolescent boys had high academic achievement than adolescent girls. There was a positive and significant relationship between emotional intelligence and academic achievement of adolescent boys and girls

2.2 STUDIES RELATED TO PARENTAL ENCOURAGEMENT

Agarwal (1989) conducted a study on the effect of Parental Encouragement upon the educational development of students. Study revealed that the urban boys received greater Parental Encouragement than the rural ones. The urban girls got greater Parental Encouragement than the rural ones. The girls in general received greater Parental Encouragement than boys.

Arora (2006) conducted study on perceived parental behavior as related to student's academic school success and competences. Study revealed that Parental acceptance and Encouragement scores were positively related with academic school success and academic competency scores.

Aggarwal (2006) conducted a study on Parental Encouragement- A panacea for student's educational development' and found that the effect of Parental Encouragement upon the academic achievement of the students would be highly significant.

Kumar (2009) found that the students who get high level of Parental Encouragement have better performance. Male and female possess different level of Parental Encouragement.

Filer & Chang (2009) examined effects of peers and Parental Encouragement to take algebra on mathematics achievement. The differential effects of racial groups and peer and parent effects on achievement were also investigated. Parent's expectations and involvement have shown significant effect on achievement of students.

Kaur (2010) found that a significant relationship between Parental Encouragement and mental health of girl students. The study reveals significant relationship between Parental Encouragement and mental health by boy students.

Gwendoline (2011) finds that education and career aspiration, socio economic status, personal ability and peer and Parental Encouragement have significant influence in the selection of nursing tertiary education in Singapore.

Sareen and Kaur (2012) revealed that there is no significant interaction between gender and Parental Encouragement with regard to physical needs, psychological needs, vocational needs. There is no difference in the Parental Encouragement of boys and girls. The study revealed that parental encouragement level was same for boys and girls.

Bhargava (2012) conducted a study to find out the impact of parental encouragement on the academic achievement of adolescents and revealed that the urban adolescent students got more Parental Encouragement than the rural adolescents. Academic level of students in urban area was higher than that of students in rural area. It showed that parental encouragement had significant and positive impact on the academic achievement of the adolescents.

Singh & Devgon (2012) studied the relationship between academic achievement and Parental Encouragement. The study revealed a positive relationship between academic achievement and Parental Encouragement. The results of the study revealed that higher the parental encouragement higher the academic achievement of the adolescents.

Kaur (2013) conducted a study to see the relationship of Study Habits of adolescents and Parental Encouragement. For this investigation, the tools used were Study Habits Inventory by MC Mukhopadhyay and D.N.Sansanwal (1983) and Parental Encouragement Scale by R.R Sharma. For conducting this study statistical techniques used were mean, standard deviation, skewness and kurtosis, Pearson's product moment correlation technique, for comparison, t-ratio has been calculated. The present study was conducted on 200 adolescents. The sample was comprised of 100 boys and 100 girl adolescents. The findings of our study revealed a significant difference between adolescent boys and girls on the variable of Study Habits. No significant difference was found between adolescent boys and girls on the variable of parental encouragement. The relationship of Study habits with parental encouragement was positive and significant.

Bhat (2013) This study explored the extent to which the self-concept and parental encouragement have the relation with academic achievement among secondary school students. The descriptive survey research method was used for the study, the sample consisted of 228 students were selected by using stratified random sampling technique. A self concept scale developed by Dr. Rastogi & Mukta Rani, and a three Dimensional Parental Behavioural Inventory designed by Hardeo Ojha on 2009 were used for data collection. Moreover for academic achievement examination marks of class 9th and 10th students obtained by them in annual examination of one previous class were noted down from the school records. The finding of the study revealed that: (i) there is a significant relationship between the self concept and academic achievement of male and female students; (II) there is no significant relationship between the father's encouragement with academic achievement of female students; (iii) there is significant relationship between the father's encouragement with academic achievement of male students; (iv) there is significant relationship between the mothers encouragement with academic achievement of both male and female students.

Sood (2013) conducted a study on study habits and attitudes of adolescents as related to parental encouragement and found inverse relationship between study habits and attitudes and parental encouragement. The study revealed that parental encouragement had negative impact on the study habits and attitudes of adolescent boys. It further revealed a significant and positive relationship between mean scores of parental encouragement and study habits and attitudes of adolescent girls. Parental encouragement was found similar for adolescent boys and girls.

2.3 HYPOTHESES OF THE STUDY

1. There exists no significant difference in parental encouragement of adolescent boys and girls.
2. There exists no significant difference in academic achievement of adolescent boys and girls.
3. A significant relationship exists between parental encouragement and academic achievement of adolescent boys.
4. A significant relationship exists between parental encouragement and academic achievement of adolescent girls.
5. A significant relationship exists between parental encouragement and academic achievement of adolescents.

CHAPTER – III

METHOD AND PROCEDURE

"Teaching is to research what method is to teaching or in sense what logic is to thinking."

- *R. Rusk*

CHAPTER – III
METHOD AND PROCEDURE

Educational research follows a systematic investigation as precisely objectively significant as possible and hence it employs scientific method & procedure as only that can lead to satisfactory results and disillusionment, It is objective, empirical and recording of controlled applications that may lead to the development of generalizations, principles and theories resulting to same extent in predictions and control of events that may be consequences and cause to specified facts but seek to integrate and systemize its findings. In the previous chapters, various reviews of related studies objectives and hypotheses were presented. In the present chapter, the research worker has to decide about the methods of data collection. The successful completion of the research work depends upon the data collected arrive at some conclusion. The present chapter is devoted to explain the outline of method and procedure and statistical techniques that had been employed for analysis and interpretation of data.

Research is purposive, scientific and a deliberate activity. Research is addition to existing knowledge. It aims at making meaningful increments to the already existing knowledge. Educational research is that which is actually directed towards development of science and behavior in educational situations. There are various methods of conducting a research study but in the present study, an appropriate method is selected keeping in view the purpose of the study, nature of the problem and kind of data necessary for its study. The selection of method and specific design with that method appropriate in investigation a research problem depends upon the kind of data that the problem entails.

However the method selected should be in harmony with specific principles and adequate enough to lead to dependable generalization. Through an appropriate method of investigation every researcher tries his best to establish genuineness, authenticity and trustworthiness of the data collected. It is necessary to adopt a systematic procedure to collect the essential data, relevant data, adequate in quality and quantity, which should also be sufficient, reliable and valid.

Any problem that of educational or scientific nature can be solved only on the basis of systematic collection of data because data are raw materials without which production in research is quite impossible. For the collection of data the investigator has to plan before hand i.e. how to conduct the identified research problem, what methodology to be employed, how sample will be selected and what statistical techniques to be administered.

The sequence of presentation involves:
1. Design of study
2. Sample
3. Tools used
4. Procedures adopted to collect data
5. Statistical techniques used for analyzing data

3.1 DESIGN OF THE STUDY

The purpose of the present study is to analyze academic achievement of adolescents in relation to Parental Encouragement. For this purpose, investigator has employed Descriptive Survey Method. This method is concerned with the surveying, description and investigation of the problem. The correlation technique was employed to study the relationship between the dependent variable and independent variable. In this present study, the dependent variable is Academic Achievement and independent variable is Parental Encouragement.

3.2 SAMPLE OF THE STUDY

The sample consists of 200 adolescents (students of 9th class) from different private schools of Hoshiarpur District.

SAMPLE DESIGN

Total Adolescents

SAMPLE DESIGN

Total students (N=200)

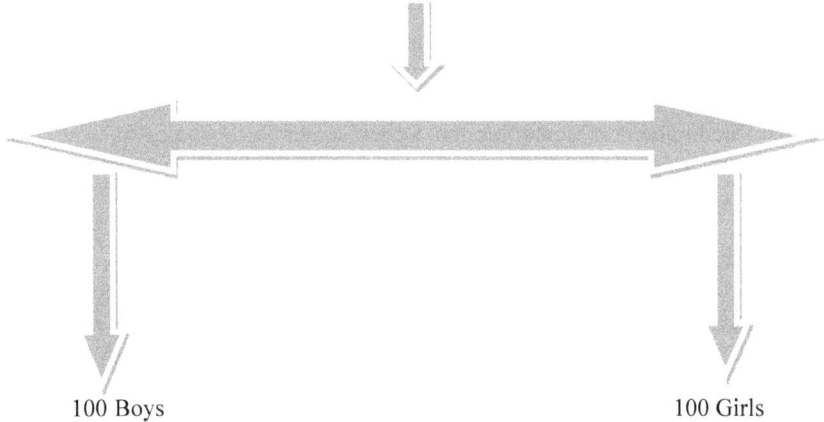

100 Boys   100 Girls

Table 3.1
Showing Break up of Total Sample

S.No	Name of the school	Boys	Girls
1.	Doaba Public Senior Secondary School, Hoshiarpur	20	20
2.	St Soldier Divine Public School, Guru Nanak Nagar, Hoshiarpur	20	20
3.	Sri Guru Harkrishan Public School, Model Town, Hoshiarpur	20	20
4	Dashmesh Public School, Mukerian, Dist. Hoshiarpur	20	20
5	Sri Guru Gobind Singh Public School, Mukerian	20	20

3.3 TOOLS USED
1. Parental Encouragement Scale (PCS) developed by R.R.Sharma's published by Psychological Corporation, Agra(2009).
2. Marks secured by students in their previous year annual examination are used to find the academic achievement.

3.4 DESCRIPTION OF THE TOOL
PARENTAL ENCOURAGEMENT SCALE (PES)

The researcher used the Parental Encouragement scale(PES) is prepared by R.R .Sharma Reader in Education, Garhwal University, Srinagar, Garwal (u.p) in 1988 and is published by National Psychological Corporation. It measures the degree of Parental Encouragement scale can be administered individually as well as in groups. There is no limit for the completion of the scale; however, ordinarily an individual student takes 25 to 30 minutes to complete it.

The Present Scale

Parental Encouragement Scale (PES) has been developed to measure degree/amount of encouragement which a child receives from his parents and also to categorize the students in terms of their Parental Encouragement. It has been designed for the student population upon higher secondary stage.

Preparation of items

In the beginning, a list of 80 items was prepared after going through available tests and other relevant literature. The list was given to five judges to ascertain the suitability and relevancy of these items for Parental Encouragement Scale.

Item Analysis

TheScale contains 50 items with three response alternatives. Their response sheets were scored. Then, the popularity value of each item was calculated by means of the following formula:

P.V. = $\dfrac{\text{Average Score of an item}}{\text{Maximum Score allotted for the item}}$

Reliability

The reliability of the scale was measured first by split half method and value was found to be 0.83. Secondly, two test-retest reliabilities were determined one after an interval of 2 weeks and other 4 weeks. The values of these two reliabilities were found to be 0.73 and 0.76 respectively. The above three sets of reliability coefficients are presented in table 3.2.

Validity

Two indices of validity of the PES were worked out as under:
1. Content Validity: the content of each item of the PES was critically examined by 5 judges, specialized in the field of education, psychology and sociology. The opinion of these judges confirmed that the PES was a sufficient valid instrument.
2. Convergent Validity: the validity of the PES was ascertained by correlating the scores of this scale with Uniyal and Aggarwal's PES. The coefficient of correlation was found to be 0.68. This indicates that the scale is a fairy valid tool.

Administration and instructions

The Parental Encouragement Scale can be administered individually as well as in group. There is no time limit for completion of the Scale; however, ordinarily an individual student takes 25 to 30 minutes to complete it.

The general instruction has been given on the title page of the scale. The test administer should read out the instructions loudly & clearly and ensure that the testees have followed them. He should also tell the testees to go through the instructions before they start marking their responses. He should explain them the mode of recording their responses the investigator should make every possible effort to see that the respondents do not consult one another while recording their responses.

Scoring Procedure

There are three responses alternatives in each item of the scale. The subject has to choose only one alternative. The marks should be allotted as follows:

Table 3.2
Scoring Procedure

Response alternatives	Socre
A	0
B	1
S	2

Thus, the total score for each item ranges from 0 to 2, whereas the grand total of the PES ranges from 0 to 80. Higher scores on the PES reveal higher amount/ degree of Parental Encouragement, whereas lower score reveal the lesser amount/ degree of encouragement.

Norms

The percentile norms are given in table in table 2 on 500 boys and 600 girls of high school classes for meaningful interpretation.

Table 3.3
Percentile norms of Parental Encouragement Scale Scores

Percentiles	Boys	Girls	Interpretation
99	79.25	79.25	
95	78.30	78.20	Very High P.E.
90	77.10	76.95	
80	74.70	74.38	
75	73.69	73.15	High P.E
70	72.73	71.90	
60	70.80	69.40	
50	68.50	66.70	
40	65.50	64.00	Average P.E
30	61.90	61.30	
25	60.90	59.55	Low P.E
20	59.25	57.00	
10	47.00	47.20	
5	32.95	42.34	Very low P.E
Mean	65.08	64.64	
S.D.	12.40	10.95	
N	500	60	

3.5 PROCEDURE FOR COLLECTING THE DATA

For the fulfillment of the requirement of the study, investigator personally selected different schools of Hoshiarpur city. The authenticity and reliability of any research is based on the collection of relevant data. For this, the tool i.e. Parental Encouragement Scale was administered to secondary school students of different schools of Hoshiarpur city. The Principals of the respective schools were requested for obtaining data from the students. The limit of data was set at 200 secondary school students of IX class from different schools that were further divided into 100 boys and 100 girls. Permission and co-operation was sought from the head of the institution for collecting data. The investigator firstly gave them general instructions for making their responses on the response sheet. All the response sheets were thoroughly checked for no item would be left out. The whole tool was completed in one sitting with no interval in between. After administering the tool, the response sheets were scored according to the directions given in the manual.

3.6 STATISTICAL TECHNIQUES USED

(i) Description of the scores presented in terms of the frequency distribution, mean, S.D., skewness and kurtosis.
(ii) For comparison, t-ratio has been calculated.
(iii) For correlation between academic achievement and parental encouragement of adolescents, Pearson's product moment correlation technique was employed.

CHAPTER – IV

ANALYSIS AND INTERPRETATION OF DATA

"Keep close to experience, add as little of your own as possible, if you have to add something, be mindful to give me account of every step you take."

- *F.M. Urban.*

CHAPTER – IV
ANALYSIS AND INTERPRETATION OF DATA

In educational research, the step that comes next to the collection of data is the analysis and interpretation of the collected data. This section is the heart of the research because it gives concise picture to the data. In other words it gives tongue to the otherwise mute data. It involves breaking down the existing complex factors into simple facts and putting the parts together in the new arrangement for the purpose of interpretation. It not only point out the important facts and relationships to give meaning to the data but also make certain generalizations about the data.

The present study was undertaken with the purpose of studying academic achievement of adolescents in relation to parental encouragement. This objective was achieved within the framework of the hypotheses mentioned in the Chapter 2. The raw data for the study was obtained with the help of survey. In order to screen the data for meaningful purpose and to test the hypotheses, the data was analyzed with the help of various statistical techniques. An attempt has been made to relate the outcome of the analysis to the framed hypotheses so as to arrive at meaningful conclusions. For the sake of convenience and keeping in view the nature and objectives of the study, the results have been presented into two sections.

Section I deals with the nature of score distribution of academic achievement and parental encouragement of adolescents to justify the application of various statistical techniques.

Section II has been dealing with the difference of means between academic achievement and parental encouragement of adolescents on the basis of gender.

Section III has been dealing with the relationship between academic achievement and parental encouragement of adolescent boys and girls.

SECTION - I
DISTRIBUTION OF SCORES

Before persisting the actual analysis of data and discussion of results pertaining to the hypotheses, it was deemed desirable to describe the nature of distribution of scores of academic achievement and parental encouragement of adolescents so as to ensure whether the condition of basic assumptions implicit in some of the statistical techniques employed here was fulfilled.

The description of scores are presented in measures of mean, median, mode, standard deviation, skewness and kurtosis in the tables 4.1 to 4.8 and figures 4.1 to 4.4

Table 4.1 Frequency Distribution of scores of Parental Encouragement of Adolescent Boys and Girls (N = 200)

Class-Interval	Boys	Girls
50-55	2	9
55-60	11	9
60-65	11	10
65-70	13	32
70-75	33	38
75-80	30	2
Total	100	100

Table 4.2 showing Mean, Median, Standard Deviation, Skewness and Kurtosis of scores of Parental Encouragement of Adolescent Boys and Girls (N = 200)

Group	Mean	Median	S.D.	Skewness	Kurtosis
Boys	69.47	72.00	7.23	-0.78	-0.72
Girls	65.58	64.00	6.51	-0.29	-0.89

The scores of parental encouragement of adolescent boys and girls were tested for normalcy. **Table 4.2** shows that:

- The values of mean and median of the scores of parental encouragement of adolescent boys as 69.47 and 72.00 respectively which are quite proximate to each other. The values of skewness and kurtosis in case of adolescent boys are -0.78 and -0.72 respectively showing the distribution as negatively skewed and platykurtic. But these distortions are quite small. Therefore the distributions can be taken as normal.
- The values of mean and median of the scores of parental encouragement of adolescent girls as 65.58 and 64.00 respectively which are quite proximate to each other. The values of skewness and kurtosis in case of adolescent boys are -0.29 and -0.89 respectively showing the distribution as negatively skewed and platykurtic. But these distortions are quite small. Therefore the distributions can be taken as normal.

Fig. 4.1 Frequency Polygon of scores of Parental Encouragement of Adolescent Boys and Girls (N = 200)

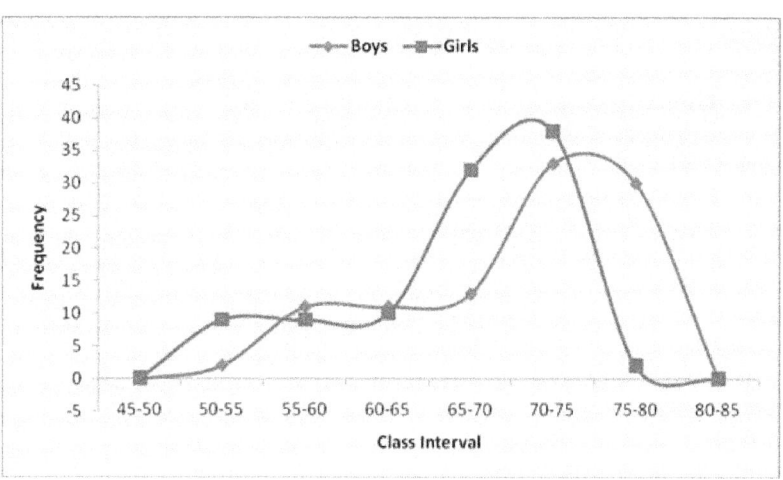

Table 4.3 Frequency Distribution of scores of Parental Encouragement of Adolescents (N = 200)

Class-Interval	Adolescents
50-55	11
55-60	20
60-65	21
65-70	45
70-75	71
75-80	32
Total	100

Table 4.4 showing Mean, Median, Standard Deviation, Skewness and Kurtosis of scores of Parental Encouragement of Adolescents (N = 200)

Group	Mean	Median	S.D.	Skewness	Kurtosis
Adolescents	67.53	70.00	7.13	-0.43	-0.99

Table 4.4 shows that:

> The values of mean and median of the scores of parental encouragement of adolescents as 67.53 and 70.00 respectively which are quite proximate to each other. The values of skewness and kurtosis in case of prospective teachers are -0.43 and -0.99 respectively showing the distribution as negatively skewed and platykurtic. But these distortions are quite small. Therefore the distributions can be taken as normal.

Fig. 4.2 Frequency Polygon of scores of Parental Encouragement of Adolescents (N = 200)

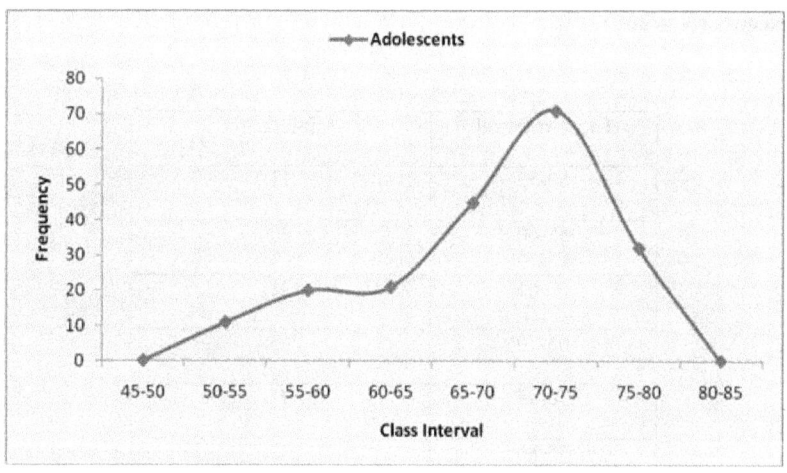

Table 4.5 Frequency Distribution of scores of Academic Achievement of Adolescent Boys and Girls (N = 200)

Class-Interval	Boys	Girls
200-250	1	0
250-300	4	0
300-350	15	5
350-400	37	6
400-450	22	16
450-500	13	26
500-550	4	31
550-600	4	16
Total	100	100

Table 4.6 showing Mean, Median, Standard Deviation, Skewness and Kurtosis of scores of Academic Achievement of Adolescent Boys and Girls (N = 200)

Group	Mean	Median	S.D.	Skewness	Kurtosis
Boys	399.63	393.00	68.14	0.48	0.68
Girls	483.37	496.50	63.54	-0.74	-0.02

The scores of academic achievement of adolescent boys and girls were tested for normalcy. **Table 4.6** shows that:

- The values of mean and median of the scores of academic achievement of adolescent boys as 399.63 and 393.00 respectively which are quite proximate to each other. The values of skewness and kurtosis in case of adolescent boys are 0.48 and 0.68 respectively showing the distribution as positively skewed and leptokurtic. But these distortions are quite small. Therefore the distributions can be taken as normal.
- The values of mean and median of the scores of academic achievement of adolescent girls as 483.37 and 496.50 respectively which are quite proximate to each other. The values of skewness and kurtosis in case of adolescent boys are -0.74 and -0.02 respectively showing the distribution as negatively skewed and platykurtic. But these distortions are quite small. Therefore the distributions can be taken as normal.

Fig. 4.3 Frequency Polygon of scores of Academic Achievement of Adolescent Boys and Girls (N = 200)

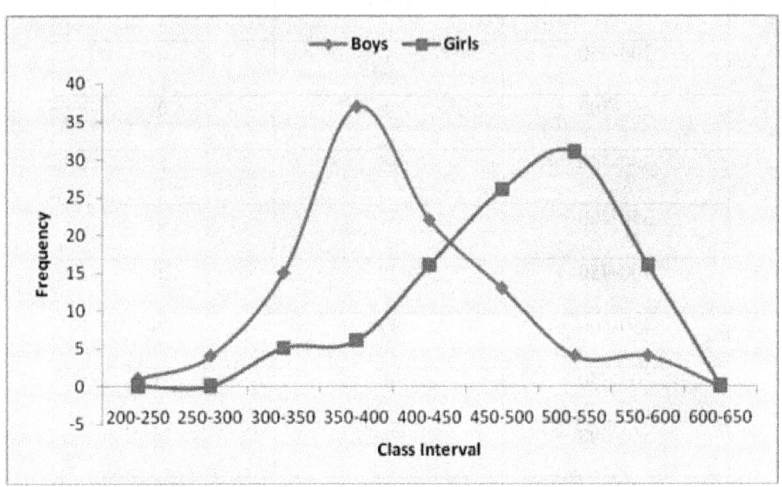

Table 4.7 Frequency Distribution of scores of Academic Achievement of Adolescents (N = 200)

Class-Interval	Adolescents
200-250	1
250-300	4
300-350	20
350-400	43
400-450	38
450-500	39
500-550	35
550-600	20
Total	100

Table 4.8 showing Mean, Median, Standard Deviation, Skewness and Kurtosis of scores of Academic Achievement of Adolescents (N = 200)

Group	Mean	Median	S.D.	Skewness	Kurtosis
Adolescents	441.50	440.50	77.98	-0.12	-0.75

Table 4.8 shows that:

➢ The values of mean and median of the scores of academic achievement of adolescents as 441.50 and 440.00 respectively which are quite proximate to each other. The values of skewness and kurtosis in case of prospective teachers are -0.12 and -0.75 respectively showing the distribution as negatively skewed and platykurtic. But these distortions are quite small. Therefore the distributions can be taken as normal.

Fig. 4.4 Frequency Polygon of scores of Academic Achievement of Adolescents (N = 200)

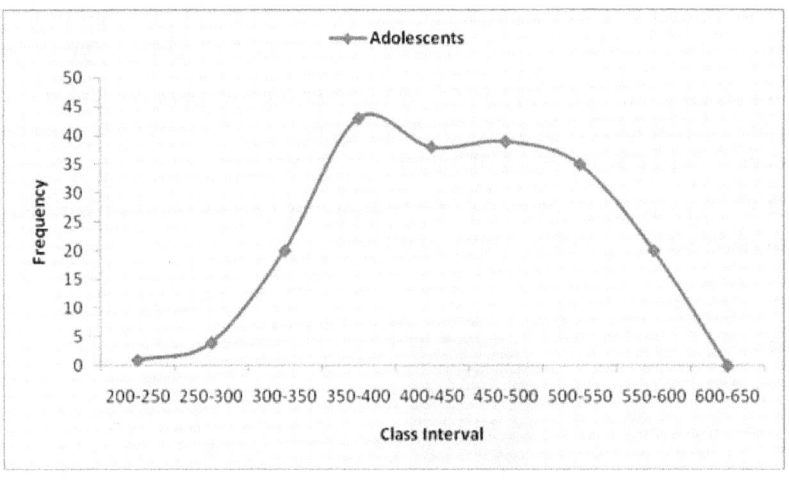

SECTION - II
SIGNIFICANCE OF DIFFERENCE OF MEANS

To investigate the significance of difference between the means, if any, of parental encouragement and academic achievement of adolescent boys and girls on the basis of gender was assessed in terms of their scores in the test in these variables and t-test was employed.

Table 4.9 Significance of the Difference between Mean Scores of Parental Encouragement of Adolescent Boys and Girls

S.No.	Group	N	M	S.D	SE_M	t-value
1.	Boys	100	69.47	7.23	0.72	4.00**
2.	Girls	100	65.58	6.51	0.65	

**significant at 0.01

Table 4.9 reveals that the mean scores of parental encouragement of adolescent boys and girls as 69.47 and 65.58 respectively and their standard deviation as 7.23 and 6.51 respectively. The t-ratio is 4.00 with $d_f = 198$ which is significant at 0.05 level of confidence. This revealed that a significant difference exists between mean scores of parental encouragement of adolescent boys and girls.

Therefore the hypothesis **1** stating that there exists no significant mean difference in the parental encouragement of adolescent boys and girls stands rejected.

As mean score on the variable of parental encouragement of adolescent boys is higher than that of adolescent girls, therefore it can further be concluded that parental encourage to boys is more than that to girls.

Fig. 4.5 Bar Graph showing Difference of Mean Scores of Parental Encouragement of Adolescent Boys and Girls

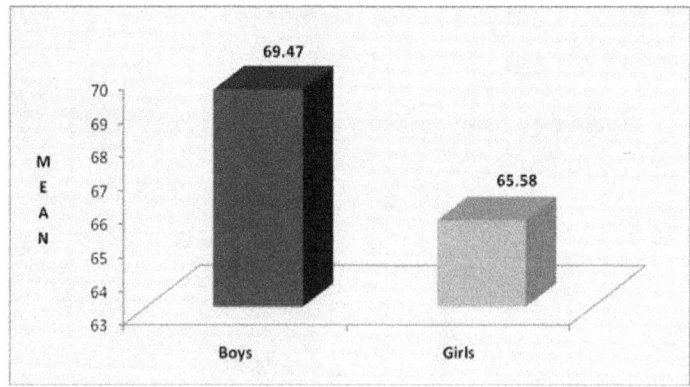

Table 4.10 Significance of the Difference between Mean Scores of Academic Achievement of Adolescent Boys and Girls

S.No.	Group	N	M	S.D	SE_M	t-value
1.	Boys	100	399.63	68.14	6.81	
2.	Girls	100	483.37	63.54	6.35	8.99**

**significant at .01 level

Table 4.10 reveals that the mean scores of academic achievement of adolescent boys and girls as 399.63 and 483.37 respectively and their standard deviation as 68.14 and 63.54 respectively. The t-ratio is 8.99 with $d_f = 198$ which is significant at 0.01 level of confidence. This revealed that a significant difference exists between mean scores of academic achievement of adolescent boys and girls.

Therefore the hypothesis **2** stating that there exists no significant mean difference in the academic achievement of adolescent boys and girls stands rejected.

As mean score on the variable of academic achievement of adolescent girls is higher than that of adolescent boys, therefore it can further be concluded that academic achievement of girls more than that of boys.

Fig. 4.6 Bar Graph showing Difference of Mean Scores of Academic Achievement of Adolescent Boys and Girls

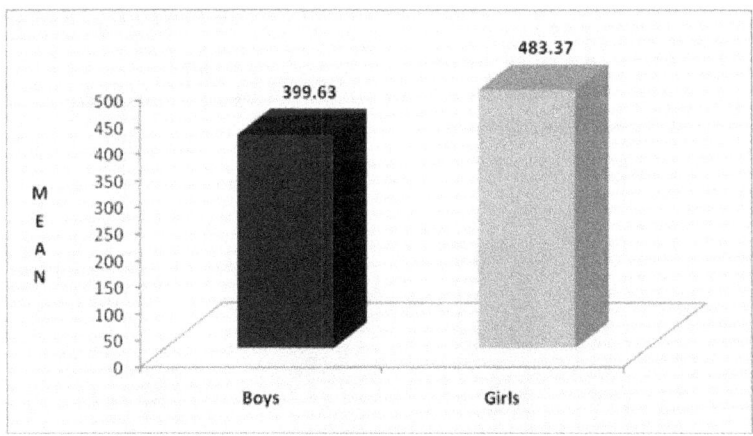

To find out the difference in the mean scores of academic achievement of adolescents with high, average and low parental encouragement, one way ANOVA was employed.

Table 4.11 Summary of Analysis of Variance for scores of Academic Achievement of Adolescents with High, Average and Low Parental Encouragement

Source of Variation	SS	d_f	MS	F-value
Between Groups	112141.31	2	56070.65	10.06**
Within groups	1097824.69	197	5572.71	
Total	1209966.00	199		

** Significant at 0.01 level

Table 4.11 depicts the F-value after comparing the groups of adolescents with high, average and low parental encouragement on the variable of academic achievement. The sum of square between the groups is 112141.31 and sum of squares within groups is 1097824.69. The F-value obtained is 10.06 which is significant at 0.01 level of confidence. It reveals that the academic achievement of adolescents with high, average and low parental encouragement differ significantly.

To find out which group of adolescents i.e. the group with high, average or low parental encouragement scored highest in their academic achievement, mean score of each group was calculated.

Table 4.12 Showing the Mean Scores of Academic Achievement of Adolescents with High, Average and Low Parental Encouragement

S. No.	Group	N	Mean
1.	High Parental Encouragement	32.00	443.66
2.	Average Parental Encouragement	131.00	454.81
3.	Low Parental Encouragement	37.00	392.51

Fig. 4.7 Showing the Mean Scores of Academic Achievement of Adolescents with High, Average and Low Parental Encouragement

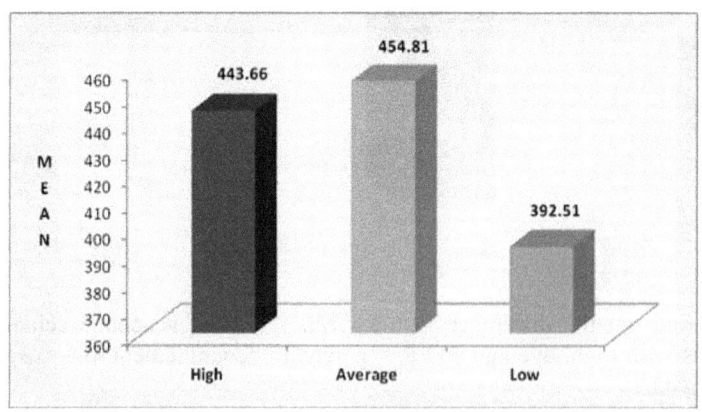

Table 4.12 and **Fig. 4.8** depicts the mean scores of academic achievement of adolescents with high parental encouragement as 443.66, that with average parental encouragement as 454.81 and with low parental encouragement as 392.51 which shows that the adolescents who have average parental encouragement achieved highest academically as compared to their other counterparts.

Hence, hypothesis **3** stating, "There exists no significant difference exists in the academic achievement of adolescents with high, average and low parental encouragement" stands rejected.

Table 4.13 Summary of Analysis of Variance for Scores of Academic Achievement of Adolescent Boys with High, Average and Low Parental Encouragement

Source of Variation	SS	d_f	MS	F-value
Between Groups	113031.27	2	56515.64	15.81**
Within groups	346648.04	97	3573.69	
Total	459679.31	99		

** Significant at 0.01 level

Table 4.13 depicts the F-value after comparing the groups of adolescent boys with high, average and low parental encouragement on the variable of academic achievement. The sum of square between the groups is 113031.27 and sum of squares within groups is 346648.04. The F-value obtained is 15.81 which is significant at 0.01 level of confidence. It reveals that the academic achievement of adolescent boys with high, average and low parental encouragement differ significantly.

To find out which group of adolescent boys i.e. the group with high, average or low parental encouragement scored highest in their academic achievement, mean score of each group was calculated.

Table 4.14 Showing the Mean Scores of Academic Achievement of Adolescent Boys with High, Average and Low Parental Encouragement

S. No.	Group	N	Mean
1	High Parental Encouragement	28	441.82
2	Average Parental Encouragement	52	398.52
3	Low Parental Encouragement	20	343.45

Fig. 4.8 Showing the Mean Scores of Academic Achievement of Adolescent boys with High, Average and Low Parental Encouragement

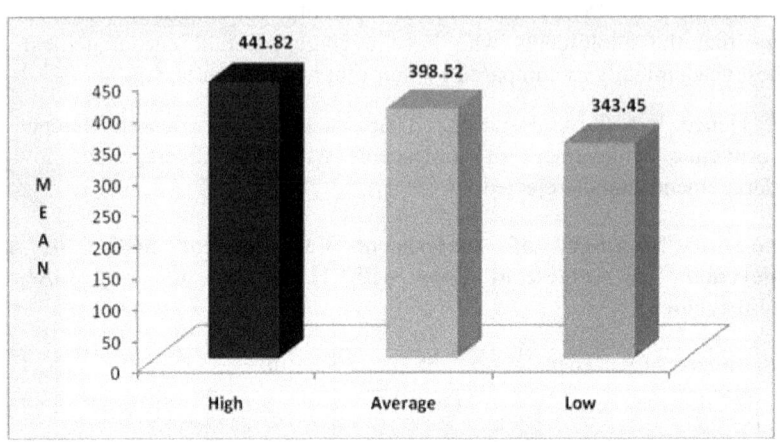

Table 4.14 and **Fig. 4.8** depicts the mean scores of academic achievement of adolescent boys with high parental encouragement as 441.82, that with average parental encouragement as 398.52 and with low parental encouragement as 343.45 which shows that the adolescent boys who have high parental encouragement achieved highest academically as compared to their other counterparts.

Hence, hypothesis **4** stating, "There exists no significant difference exists in the academic achievement of adolescent boys with high, average and low parental encouragement" stands rejected.

Table 4.15 Summary of Analysis of Variance for Scores of Academic Achievement of Adolescent Girls with High, Average and Low Parental Encouragement

Source of Variation	SS	d_f	MS	F-value
Between Groups	39642.71	2	19821.36	5.34**
Within groups	360024.60	97	3711.59	
Total	399667.31	99		

** Significant at 0.01 level

Table 4.15 depicts the F-value after comparing the groups of adolescent girls with high, average and low parental encouragement on the variable of academic achievement. The sum of square between the groups is 39642.71 and sum of squares within groups is 360024.60. The F-value obtained is 5.34 which is significant at 0.01 level of confidence. It reveals that the academic achievement of adolescent girls with high, average and low parental encouragement differ significantly.

To find out which group of adolescent girls i.e. the group with high, average or low parental encouragement scored highest in their academic achievement, mean score of each group was calculated.

Table 4.16 Showing the Mean Scores of Academic Achievement of Adolescent Girls with High, Average and Low Parental Encouragement

S. No.	Group	N	Mean
1	High Parental Encouragement	22	509.86
2	Average Parental Encouragement	59	484.95
3	Low Parental Encouragement	19	447.79

Fig. 4.9 Showing the Mean Scores of Academic Achievement of Adolescent girls with High, Average and Low Parental Encouragement

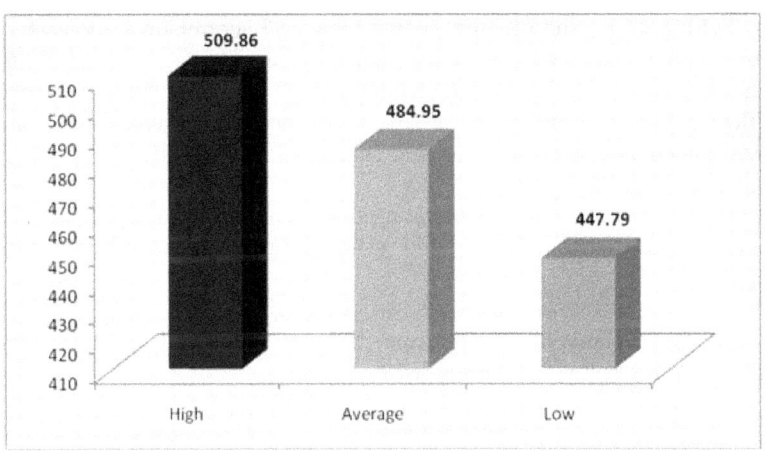

Table 4.16 and **Fig. 4.9** depicts the mean scores of academic achievement of adolescent girls with high parental encouragement as 509.86, that with average parental encouragement as 484.95 and with low parental encouragement as 447.79 which shows that the adolescent girls who have high parental encouragement achieved highest academically as compared to their other counterparts.

Hence, hypothesis **5** stating, "There exists no significant difference exists in the academic achievement of adolescent girls with high, average and low parental encouragement" stands rejected.

SECTION – III

COEFFICIENT OF CORRELATION

As the present study is intended to find out the relationship between academic achievement and parental encouragement of adolescents, Pearson's Product Moment correlation technique was employed.

Table 4.17 Coefficient of Correlation between Parental Encouragement and Academic Achievement of Adolescents

Category	N	R
Adolescent Boys	100	0.36**
Adolescent Girls	100	0.44**
Total Adolescents	200	0.18*

**significant at 0.01 level   *significant at 0.05 level

Table 4.17 shows the coefficient of correlation between parental encouragement and academic achievement of adolescent boys as 0.36; that of adolescent girls as 0.44 and of total adolescents as 0.18, all of which are positive and significant. This indicates that a significant positive relationship exist between parental encouragement and academic achievement of adolescent boys, adolescent girls and adolescents.

Therefore the hypothesis **6** stating that there exists no significant relationship between parental encouragement and academic achievement of adolescents stands rejected.

Fig 4.10 Coefficient of Correlation between Parental Encouragement and Academic Achievement of Adolescents

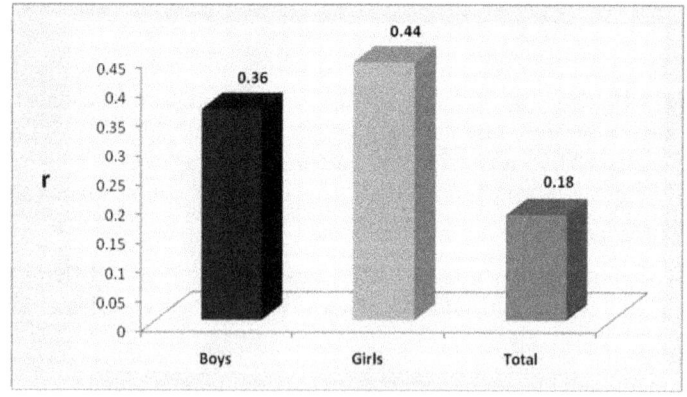

4.2 CONCLUSIONS

On the basis of the above discussions, the following conclusions can be drawn:

1. A significant difference exists between mean scores of parental encouragement of adolescent boys and girls. As mean score on the variable of parental encouragement of adolescent boys is higher than that of adolescent girls, therefore it can further be concluded that parental encourage to boys is more than that to girls.

2. A significant difference exists between mean scores of academic achievement of adolescent boys and girls. As mean score on the variable of academic achievement of adolescent girls is higher than that of adolescent boys, therefore it can further be concluded that academic achievement of girls more than that of boys.

3. The academic achievement of adolescents with high, average and low parental encouragement was found differ significantly. Also it is found that the adolescents who have average parental encouragement achieved highest academically as compared to their other counterparts.

4. The academic achievement of adolescent boys with high, average and low parental encouragement was found differ significantly. Also it is found that the adolescent boys who have high parental encouragement achieved highest academically as compared to their other counterparts.

5. The academic achievement of adolescent girls with high, average and low parental encouragement was found differ significantly. Also it is found that the adolescent girls who have high parental encouragement achieved highest academically as compared to their other counterparts.

6. A significant positive relationship exists between parental encouragement and academic achievement of adolescent boys, adolescent girls and adolescents.

CHAPTER – V

SUMMARY AND CONCLUSIONS

"Not only has a good summary served as a time saver. It can help any novice to better understand the conclusions, recommendations and generalizations derived from data analysis".

- *M.H.MC. Asham.*

CHAPTER – V
SUMMARY AND CONCLUSIONS

5.1 INTRODUCTION

It is a well known fact that education is as old as the human race itself. Since its inception, it has undergone a number of phases and revolutions. It's a never-ending process of inner growth and development which starts right from the conceiving of life till the end of it. In this rapidly changing world of science and technology, the role of education has become vital. It is appropriately regarded as the key to national prosperity and welfare and is the most important form of national investment. Education is the complete development of the individuality of the child, so that he can make an original contribution to human life according to the best of his capability and capacity. Education, in real sense, is to humanize humanity and to make life progressive, cultured and civilized.

Creation of god is so beautiful that we cannot express it in words. It is like the sugar for blind. Parents are the best creation of God. In the lap of parents, children forget all pain and grief of this world. Every child feels protected with his parents. After birth every child moves forward at his path of life with the help of his parents at every step. The blessings of parents are always with their children. Behind every successful person there is always support and help of parents. One can never achieve his/her destination without the guidance of parents. When a person look backward, he/ she realize that it's wholly the parents support and encouragement what he/ she achieves in life. Every great man has the encouragement of parents behind him.

5.1.1 ADOLESCENCE

Adolescence, no doubt, is the most important period of human life but at the same time it is the most critical period of an individual's development. Adolescence is the phase of development and adjustment, being the traditional period between childhood and adulthood. It is the transitional period in everybody's life, which begins at the end of childhood and closes at the beginning of adulthood. Biologically, adolescence is the age when puberty draws. Chronologically this is a span of life ranging from 12 to 19 years.

The term 'adolescence' comes from the word 'adolescere' which means 'to grow' or 'to grow to maturity'. Maturity not only evolves physical but also mental growth. On the physical side, it means attainment of a mature individual and development of the sex apparatus to make procreation possible. Mentally a mature individual is one whose intelligence has reached its maximum growth. In fact, adolescence period is the time when individuals grow to maturity sexually, intellectually, socially and emotionally. During the phase of adolescence, the individual is neither a child nor a grown up. An adolescent is emotionally unstable during this period. They can't hide their feelings; give expression to their feelings at the right time and in a proper manner. Adolescence is the transitional period from dependence on parents to self-sufficient childhood.

The term adolescence has a broader meaning these days than it had in early years. The adolescent's task is not simply to interact with the external environment or with other individuals but also to develop its own potentialities. They try to expose their role in the world in which they live. It is a stage of new experiences, responsibilities and new relationships with adults as well as peers, which influence his personality, his ability to emerge out of conflicting situations and his futuristic patterns of life.

Psychologically adolescence is a marginal situation, which involves psychological disturbances and problems of adjustment. It differentiates the childhood behavior from adulthood behavior. This period of adolescence, in general, offers an individual a large variety of new experiences and at same time usually finds him less prepared to meet challenges than at any other stage. It has been called a period of stress and strain, storm and strife as all capacities physiological as well as psychological are reaching at a peak.

Harlock (1976) states, "Adolescence is both a way of life and span of time in the physical and psychological development of an individual. It represents a period of growth and change in nearly all aspects of child's physical, mental, social and emotional life. It is the time of new experiences, new responsibilities and new relationships with adults as well as peers."

Collins Cob Wild English Language Dictionary (1991) defines, "Adolescence is the period of one's life in which one develops from being a child into being an adult."

New Illustrated Webster's Dictionary (1992) states, "Adolescence is the process of going up the stage or period of growth from the onset of puberty to the stage to adult development."

According to Oxford English Dictionary (1993), "Adolescence is the process or condition of growing from child to manhood or womanhood, the period of growing up."

According to Chamber's 21st Century Dictionary (1999), "Adolescent is said to be of a young person at the stage of development between adulthood and childhood or between puberty and adulthood."

Dictionary of Psychology (2001) states," Adolescence is a period of development from onset of puberty to attainment of adulthood." given to assessment and examination.

In this rapidly changing world and with growing advancement in science and technology, the place of education has become so vital that every parent today sets high goals to educate his/her child. Parents want the child to shine in academics no matter at what cost! Teacher also sees children's examination performance as measure of their own worth. The test scores, marks or grades assigned to the pupils on the basis of his performance in the achievement tests determine his status with respect to attained skill or knowledge compared with other pupils and also with the adopted standard of the school.

5.1.2 ACADEMIC ACHIEVEMENT

Modern society is achievement oriented. Academic achievement is the point and center of educational growth and development. It is the most important goal of education. Despite many varied statements about aims of education, the academic achievement of people continues to be the primary and the most important goal of education. Academic achievement creates a challenge for every pupil at all levels of education. It is the status or level of a person's learning and his capability to apply what he has learnt. Academic achievement is the core of a wider term i.e. educational growth, which means growth in all aspects. The assessment of academic achievement has been largely confined to the evaluation in terms of information, knowledge and understanding.

In literal sense, the term 'Academic Achievement' is the combination of two words: Academic + Achievement. It implies 'scholarly accomplishment'. The term 'Academic' has been derived from the term 'Academy' which means a school where special types of instructions are imparted. 'Achievement' means one's learning attainment, accomplishment and proficiency of performance. It refers to the pupil's knowledge attained and skills developed in the school subjects which are assessed by the authorities with the help of achievement tests.

Thus, Academic Achievement in general refers to the degree or level of success or proficiency attained in some specific areas concerning scholastic academic work. Academic achievement plays a significant role in almost all aspects of human life, in shaping the career of an individual and planning for future education. It encourages the students to work hard and learn more. It forms the basis of admission and promotion in a class. Achievement is generally used in the sense of "ability to do, capacity to do or tendency to do" **(Monore and Engelhard, 1952)**. But a person's performance is conditioned by the circumstances, abilities and capacities.

Academic achievement is the achievement related to academic performance. **Good (1974)** defined academic achievement as the knowledge attained or skills developed in the school subjects usually through test scores or there after marks assigned by teacher or both.

According to Oxford Advanced Learner's Dictionary (2000), "Achievement is the thing that somebody has done successfully, especially using his/her effort and skill."

Kumari (2001) defined academic achievement as the sum total of information gained after completing a course of instruction particularly or fully in a particular grade that he has obtained on an achievement test."

According to Merriam Webster's Collegiate Dictionary (2001), "Achievement is an art of achieving a result gained by efforts; the quality and quantity of students work."

According to Ollendik (2003), "Academic Achievement is defined as the knowledge and skills that an individual learns through direct instruction. Achievement tests measure what a person has learned, where an aptitude test (including that of intelligence) assess a person's potential for learning."

According To Subramanyam (2008), "Education achievement is usually defined in three ways; the grades the students earn in school, their performance and standardized tests of academic achievement or the number of years of schooling completed."

Academic achievement is the accomplishment or proficiency of performance in a given skill or body of knowledge. It means the amount of knowledge gained by the student in different subjects of study. Academic achievement is the act of achieving or furnishing something that has been attained successfully especially by means of skills, perseverance or practice. Academic achievement is related to the acquisition of principles, generalizations and the capacity to perform efficiently (certain manipulations of objects, symbols and ideas). Assessment of academic performance has been largely confirmed to the evaluation in terms of information, knowledge and understanding. It is universally accepted that the acquisition of factual data is not an end in itself but an individual who has received education should show evidence of having understood them. For obvious reason the examinations are largely confined to the measurement of the amount of information which students have acquired. It is perhaps the only expected basis for promotion or to fulfill the requirement for any degree or diploma. It is the actual or assumed possession of knowledge that counts either for admission into a class or course.

According to Oxford Advanced Learner's Dictionary (2000), "Achievement is the thing that somebody has done successfully, especially using his/her effort and skill."

Kumari (2001) defined academic achievement as the sum total of information gained after completing a course of instruction particularly or fully in a particular grade that he has obtained on an achievement test."

According to Merriam Webster's Collegiate Dictionary (2001), "Achievement is an art of achieving a result gained by efforts; the quality and quantity of students work."

According to Ollendik (2003), "Academic Achievement is defined as the knowledge and skills that an individual learns through direct instruction. Achievement tests measure what a person has learned, where an aptitude test (including that of intelligence) assess a person's potential for learning."

According To Subramanyam (2008), "Education achievement is usually defined in three ways; the grades the students earn in school, their performance and standardized tests of academic achievement or the number of years of schooling completed."

Academic achievement is the accomplishment or proficiency of performance in a given skill or body of knowledge. It means the amount of knowledge gained by the student in different subjects of study. Academic achievement is the act of achieving or furnishing something that has been attained successfully especially by means of skills, perseverance or practice. Academic achievement is related to the acquisition of principles, generalizations and the capacity to perform efficiently (certain manipulations of objects, symbols and ideas). Assessment of academic performance has been largely confirmed to the evaluation in terms of information, knowledge and understanding. It is universally accepted that the acquisition of factual data is not an end in itself but an individual who has received education should show evidence of having understood them. For obvious reason the examinations are largely confined to the measurement of the amount of information which students have acquired. It is perhaps the only expected basis for promotion or to fulfill the requirement for any degree or diploma. It is the actual or assumed possession of knowledge that counts either for admission into a class or course.

5.1.3 PARENTAL ENCOURAGEMENT

Parental encouragement is important in shaping attitude, values, self confidence and behavior of child. It refers to the treatment originating from parents towards the child with a view to enhance the possibilities, if future occurrences of good behavior by care, concern, approval and guidance.

Parental Encouragement is one of the aspects of parent's treatment patterns. The parents help the child, guide him and coax him so that he may not feel disheartened at a particular point of difficulty. The entire treatment may have many individual traits. But contents and directions are the same i.e. to give encouragement to the child. It may be in form of approval or may be in the form of asking the child to modify his behavior in the child which amounts to discouragements. Parental encouragement, as a term in education, has very explicitly has been defined by *Rossi* in these words:

> *"When father and mother approve or appreciate any activity related to education or revoke any hurdle felt by the student in the process, or guide him the right and wrong - this entire spectrum activity comes within the purview of "Parental Encouragement".*

According to Chaube (1983) "If the individual is not having proper parental encouragement, he may develop complexes. This makes him mal- adjusted in life in various ways. The parental encouragement is not only important for individual development but for the future life also. Thus parental encouragement is the backbone of the adolescent's personal life."

According to Sharma (1988), "Parental Encouragement is the treatment of originating from parents towards the child with a view to enhance the possibilities of the future occurrence of good behavior by care, concern, approval and guidance."

According to Thomson (1989) "Mother has more opportunity than the father to influence her child's psychological group and behavior. Tradition also favors' the mother's influence since child rearing in our culture is generally recognized as primarily mother's privilege and responsibility.'

Oxford Advanced Learner Dictionary(1989) states, "Parental Encouragement is referred to ones father or mother encouragement means is given to support confidence or hope, to encouragement means action of encouraging shows of encouragement thing that encourages."

According to Grolnick and slowiaczek(1994) defined that parental involvement as the allocation of resources to the child's academic endeavor.

The family is the oldest, basic and fundamental unit of human society. It consists of the husband, wife, children together with all the young and all dependents. They are related to one another is one way or the other. Thus family may be regarded as a small social group consisting of a few related persons. In our country, in family parents are considered as God. God is the supreme power in the world. Parents are the best creation of the creator, every child feels protected in lap of his parents. After his birth every child moves forward at his path of life and gets help of his parents at every step. He always finds their blessings, hands on his head. Every successful person after reaching his destination finds that his success is because of the help of his bringing up finds that these were his parents who has been performing a great role to make the life a success. They shine like sun on the sky of this world. Every great man and child has encouragement of their parents behind their success. Soldiers, who are fighting at the border and destroy the troops of enemies of their country, they say, destroy! The enemies of your mother India always raise high." Thus children have the encouragement of their parents behind them.

From the time of birth, child's personality is molded by the family in which he lives. If the child finds a healthy environment at home he has all chances for development of all round personality. It is not the number of family members which is being observed in many cases. Present families are able to inculcate many values in their members. Even two individuals of the same family do not get same home environment& encouragement.

The parents seem to play a very important role in molding their children character, personality, career and advancement in education. They may differently devote their attention, time and efforts to different domains such as child's social, religious activities, academics and athletics i.e. traditional phase of growth and development between childhood and adulthood.

The term "Parental Encouragement" refers to the treatment originating from parents towards the child with a view to enhance the possibilities if future occurrences of good behavior by care, concern, approval and guidance. Parental Encouragement is one of the aspects of parent treatment patterns. The parents help the child, guide him and coax him so that he may not feel disheartened at a particular point of difficulty. The entire treatment may have many individual traits. But their contents and directions are the same .i.e. to give encouragement to the child. It may be in the form of approval or may be in the form of asking in the child to modify his behavior. In case, it creates avoidance behavior in the child which amounts to discouragement. Parental Encouragement is of great significance in developing psychological as well as academic behavior of a child.

5.2 STATEMENT OF THE STUDY
A STUDY OF ACADEMIC ACHIEVEMENT OF ADOLESCENTS IN RELATION TO PARENTAL ENCOURAGEMENT

5.3 OPERATIONAL DEFINITIONS OF THE TERMS USED
ACADEMIC ACHIEVEMENT

Academic Achievement refers to the pupil's knowledge attained and skills developed in the school subjects which are assessed by the authorities with the help of achievement tests. Academic Achievement in general refers to the degree or level of success or proficiency attained in some specific areas concerning scholastic academic work.

PARENTAL ENCOURAGEMENT

Parental Encouragement refers to the treatment originating from parents towards the child with a view to enhance the possibilities of future occurrences of good behavior by care, concern, approval and guidance.

5.4 OBJECTIVES OF THE STUDY

The following were the objectives laid down for the present study:
1. To study and compare parental encouragement of adolescent boys and girls.
2. To study and compare academic achievement of adolescent boys and girls.
3. To study the relationship between parental encouragement and academic achievement of adolescent boys and girls.

5.5 HYPOTHESES OF THE STUDY

1. There exists no significant difference in parental encouragement of adolescent boys and girls.
2. There exists no significant difference in academic achievement of adolescent boys and girls.
3. A significant relationship exists between parental encouragement and academic achievement of adolescent boys.
4. A significant relationship exists between parental encouragement and academic achievement of adolescent girls.
5. A significant relationship exists between parental encouragement and academic achievement of adolescents.

5.6 NEED AND SIGNIFICANCE OF THE STUDY

Children are the most important asset of a country. It is they who will become tomorrow's young men and will provide the human potential required for the country's development. It is therefore necessary that today's child should be healthy both physically and mentally so that tomorrow he may prove to be an energetic and dynamic young man. School education is an important segment of the total educational system contributing significantly to the individual as well as to national development. A good school provides environment conducive for development of cognitive, affective and psychomotor domains for all round development of individual.

An achievement test is a measure of an individual's degree of accomplishment or learning in a subject or task. The achievement test serves as a tool to measure current knowledge levels for the purpose of placing students in an educational environment where they have the chance to advance at a pace that is suitable for their abilities. The assessment of academic achievement also provides feedback both to teachers and parents. It helps the teachers to know whether the teaching methods are effective or not and helps them in bringing improvement accordingly. In the world today, where knowledge is being multiplied exponentially, education is not justifying itself by remaining merely contented with the objective of imparting of certain amount of knowledge but should help to improve the quality of life. One is to acquire knowledge; other is to acquire the ability the ability to use knowledge. Life is becoming complex day by day. In the present scenario youth as well as children are facing difficulties. It has been observed that the families and communities are important in helping youth develop their knowledge and skills, to make them emotionally mature so that they can obtain technologically sophisticated jobs which are emerging part of the society.

Academic achievement plays an important role in the life of the child and helps to elevate the social economics status of individual as well as family. Parental Encouragement plays a supporting role in habit formation & personality development of an individual specifically in case of adolescence. It is the stage where maximum growth and development of adolescence take place.

Today, adolescents live in a society which has become multi-complex, thus making the roles of adolescents very diffuse and confusing. The roles of adolescents and their development, as tasks are no longer well defined and prescribed. Knowledge explosion, material wealth pursuit, plurality of society and estrangement from the extended family system, the hypocrisy of adult standards and the fallacy of physical maturity all present a great battle for adolescents to fight with the dilemma of indefinite status. They are facing problems like peer pressure and competition, adjustments at home and society, in general making them frustrated which affect their academic achievement. Good academic achievement of adolescents directly related or depends upon parental encouragement. Thus, investigator attempts to study how academic achievement of adolescents is affected by parental encouragement.

5.7 DESIGN OF THE STUDY

The purpose of the present study was to analyze Academic Achievement among adolescents in relation to Parental Encouragement. For this purpose, investigator has employed Descriptive Survey Method. This method is concerned with the surveying, description and investigation of the problem. Pearsons' Coefficient of Correlation technique was employed to study the relationship between the variables. T ratio was employed to find out the differences between the means. In this present study, the dependent variable was Academic Achievement and independent variable was Parental Encouragement.

5.8 SAMPLE

A sample of 200 students of 9th class (100 boys and 100 girls) was selected from private schools of Hoshiarpur District.

5.9 TOOLS USED
1. Parental Encouragement Scale (PCS) developed by R.R.Sharma's published by Psychological Corporation, Agra(2009).
2. Marks secured by students in their previous year annual examination are used to find the academic achievement.

5.10 STATISTICAL TECHNIQUES USED
1. Descriptive statistical techniques like mean and standard deviation.
2. Correlation is used to find out the relationship
3. t- Test is employed to check the significance of difference between means.

5.11 CONCLUSIONS
On the basis of the above discussions, the following conclusions were drawn:
1. A significant difference exists between mean scores of parental encouragement of adolescent boys and girls. As mean score on the variable of parental encouragement of adolescent boys is higher than that of adolescent girls, therefore it can further be concluded that parental encourage to boys is more than that to girls.
2. A significant difference exists between mean scores of academic achievement of adolescent boys and girls. As mean score on the variable of academic achievement of adolescent girls is higher than that of adolescent boys, therefore it can further be concluded that academic achievement of girls more than that of boys.
3. The academic achievement of adolescents with high, average and low parental encouragement was found differ significantly. Also it is found that the adolescents who have average parental encouragement achieved highest academically as compared to their other counterparts.
4. The academic achievement of adolescent boys with high, average and low parental encouragement was found differ significantly. Also it is found that the adolescent boys who have high parental encouragement achieved highest academically as compared to their other counterparts.
5. The academic achievement of adolescent girls with high, average and low parental encouragement was found differ significantly. Also it is found that the adolescent girls who have high parental encouragement achieved highest academically as compared to their other counterparts.
6. A significant positive relationship exists between parental encouragement and academic achievement of adolescent boys, adolescent girls and adolescents.

5.12 EDUCATIONAL IMPLICATIONS
Research work will not be consider complete in itself until research findings are put to some practical use, as such in this action of the chapter an attempt is made to see how the findings of the present study can be used as guidelines to pamper, to protect and to promote the academic achievement of the adolescents.

The study in hand has come out with certain revealing findings, which if given due care and proper consideration with children in one way or the other will certainly help a lot in developing desirable habits both among the adults and children. In other words, it needs a very healthy participation on the part of parents, the children, the family members, he teachers and the society. It will help bridge the gap between child's needs and prevalent practices. As such, the following suggestions if their true spirit will really work, accepted in desired form and practiced in their true spirit will really work wonders in making the children aspire realistically achieve highly and adjust with their environment.

School education is an important segment of the total educational system contributing significantly to the individual as well as to national development. Human potential can be created and improved with the help of education system. Present study seeks to find out such implications for the betterment of the children through education. It is a hard fact that their aspiring high will carry no meaning and neither their achievement will be put to any use because the one who himself has poor academic achievement naturally can't contribute anything to the enlightenment and enrichment or the society. It is matter of great concern that there is an abysmal gulf between the academic achievement of the adolescent girls and the boys. The responsibility to enhance the academic achievement rests squarely on the shoulders of the parents in general and mothers in particular at home and teachers in the classroom. The parents have to work as a guide to help them against the ups and down of the life. It is a time when parents need to involve in their children's academic achievement with their encouragement. If education is considered to be education of four H's Head, Heart, Hand and Health, then parents need to be contributing in the development of all these. The present research revealed a significant difference in the academic achievement of adolescent boys and girls. The mean score of girls is found high on the variable academic achievement. The study suggests motivating the boys for high achievement in academics.

The study in hand was conducted to find out the differences in the parental encouragement of students in their academic achievement. A significant and positive difference is found in the parental encouragement as the mean score of boys is found high than their counterparts revealing that parents encouraged boys more than girls. The results of the present work suggest that parents should also encourage their daughters to take part in every field of life, as no field is now untouched by women.

The results of present study also revealed that the adolescents who have average parental encouragement achieved higher academically as compared to their other counterparts having higher or lower parental encouragement. Also it was found that the adolescent boys and girls who have high parental encouragement achieved highest academically as compared to their other counterparts having average or low parental encouragement. Therefore, the parents should keep on encouraging their children in taking independent decisions wisely, taking part in various curricular and co curricular activities. Parents should encourage their children to perform better in their studies. They should provide all the facilities for the educational and psychological development of the child. Parents should reward their students when they perform better in any field. Parents should make every effort to give them congenial and conducive environment so that they may improve their achievement academically. Hence, the present study has multiple implications in the field of psychology and education. The findings of the study can become an important source of information and guidance for the parents and teachers to encourage their children in a proper way.

5.13 SUGGETIONS FOR FURTHER RESEARCH

1. The sample for the present research was taken from different schools of Hoshiarpur. In order to give more conclusive results, this study can be undertaken on a larger population spread over a larger area and on a longitudinal basis.
2. Since the focus of the present study is children of 9th class, similar study can be conducted on children of other age groups.
3. Further a comparative research can be conducted to find out the academic achievement and parental encouragement of adolescents from parents in service sector with those having their own business.
4. Similarly Academic Achievement may be studied in relation to other variables like values, attitude, creativity, emotional aspiration and study habits etc.
5. A comparative study may be carried out to study the Academic Achievement and Parental Encouragement of government and private urban and rural area adolescents.

BIBLIOGRAPHY

Agarwal, K.L. (1989). A study of the effect of parental encouragement upon the educational development of students. Ph.D. Education, Garwal University, *Fifth Survey of Research in Education*, 2.

Aggarwal, K.L. (1990). Educational development of students of secondary stage; the effect of parental encouragement. *Indian Educational Review*, xxv (4), 67-70.

Agrawal, K. L. and Pande, S. K. (1997). Influence of parental encouragement on educational achievement of students. *Indian Journal of Psychometry and Education*, 28,(1)59-61.

Ahuja and Blench,A. (2004). Socialized personality achievement, exploring the links european *Journal and Psychological Assesment*, 20 (3).

Anderson, J.P. (1965). *The relationship between certain aspects of parental behaviour and attitudes of junior high school pupils*. New York Teacher College Columbia University.

Asthana, M. (2011). Self-concept, mental ability and scholastic achievement of secondary school students of Varanasi. *Journal of Community Guidance & Research*, 28, (1)82-88.

Augustine, J. (2010). Teaching aptitude, competency, academic background and achievement in educational psychology. *Edutracks*, .9, (6) 26-27.

Bamman, S. S. and Ksheersagar, S. (2008). Self-concept and academic achievement among students. *Indian Journal of Psychometry and Education*, 39, (1)57-59.

Bhat, A.M. (2013). Academic achievement of secondary school students in relation to self-concept and parental encouragement. *International Journal of Recent Scientific Research*,

Bhullar.M. (2006). *Academic achievement in socio-economic status and parental encouragement*. M.ed Dissertation, Panjab university, Chandigarh.

Chen, Xinyin; Li (2012). *Dan Journal of Family Psychology*, 26(6), 927-936. doi: 10.1037/a0030708.

Crow, L.D. and Crow. (1969). *Adolescent development and Adjustment*. United States: Mc Grow – Hill Book Company.

Ergene.T.(2011). The relationships among test anxiety, study habits, achievement motivation and academic performance among Turkish high school students. *Education and Science*, 36 (160).

Fan, X. and Chen, M. (2001). Parental involvement and students' academic achievement: A meta-analysis. *Educational Psychology Review*, 13, (1)1-22.

Farzana (2011). Impact of birth order on academic achievement of high school students. *Edutracks*, 11, (2)39-40.

Fatima, I., Ghayas, S. and Adil, A. (2012). Impact of achievement goals, sociability and gender on academic achievement of university students. *Journal of the Indian Academy of Applied Psychology*, 38,(2)374-384.

Garette, E. (1981). *Statistics is Psychology and Education*. Vakilis, Feffer and Simons Limited, Bombay.

Gelat, V.K. (1999). A study of effect of study habits on English achievement at secondary level. *Journal Research and Extention*, 9 (3).

Good, C.V. (1973). *Dictionary of Education*. New York, London: McGraw Hill Book Co.Inc,.

Gwendoline C.L,Kuick. T, Yong .K. (2011). The Mediating Effects of Peer and Parental Encouragement on Student's Choice of a Nursing. *Education Journal of Applied Business and Management Studies,* 2(1): ISSN: 2010-0949.

Hemamalini, H.C. (2011). Anxiety and academic achievement of high school students of Mysore city. *Journal of Community Guidance & Research*, 28, (1)94-98.

Kapil, N. and Gupta, A. S. (2011). Stress management techniques and academic performance among adolescents. *Indian Journal of Psychometry and Education,* 42, (1) 51-54.

Kasinath, H. M. (2003). Piagetian conservation abilities as determinants of academic achievement. *Journal of Indian Education,* XXIX, (1088-92.

Kaul, L. (2007). *Methodology of Educational Research*. Vikas Publication House, New Delhi.

Kaur Rrupinderjit (2003). *Study habits as determinants of academic achievement in science.* M.Ed dissertation, Panjab university, Chandigarh

Kaur, J. and Singh, G. (2011) Study of academic achievement in relation to emotional intelligence of adolescents. Researcher's Tandem, 2, (5)50-55.

Kaur, R . (2009) .*A study of academic achievement of adolescents in relation to academic stress.* M.Ed. Dissertation, Panjab University Chandigarh.

Kaur. I. (2013). *Academic achievement of adolescents in relation to academic achievement motivation and study habits.* M.ed Dissertation, Panjab university, Chandigarh.

Kumar, V., Srivastava, P. and Aggarwal, N. M. (2009) Study habits and academic achievement of the students at secondary level. *Behavioural Scientist,* 10,(2), 157-160.

*Kumar,*Mukesh. *(2012)* a comparative study of the parental encouragement between art and science senior secondary students in relation to their academic achievement, *International Journal of Education and Research* 69, 1(IV) ISSN:2277-1255

Lakshmi.R, Aishwariya & Arora, Meenakshi (2006). *Perceived Parental behaviour as related to student's academic school success and competence.* Ph.D.Psychology, Panjab university, Chandigarh.

Lodi, A. K. and Tyagi, V. (2008). Exploration of the impact of social intelligence on academic achievement. *Vivek Journal of Education and Research,* 1(1), 102-109.

Marsh, H.W. and Yeung, A. S. (1997) Causal effects of academic self-concept on academic achievement: Structural equation models of longitudinal data. *Journal of Educational Psychology,* 89(1), 41-54.

Moses C. Ossai (2012). Age and gender differences in study habits: A framework for proactive counselling against low academic achievement, *ISSN 2240-0524 Journal of Educational and Social Research, 2 (3)2,*67.

Norman, B. (1995). Predicting antisocial behavior in youngsters displaying poor academic achievement: A review of risk factors. *Journal of Developmental and Behavioral Pediatrics,* 16,(4)271-276.

Ogbodo R.O. (2002). *Effective study habits and examination guide for students,* Gracehand Publishers Abuja.

Osa-Edoh.G.I, and Alutu.A.N.G. (2012). A survey of students study habits in selected secondary schools:implication for counselling, *Current Research Journal of Social Sciences* 4(3): 228-234, 2012 ISSN: 2041-3246© Maxwell Scientific Organization,

Pannu, R. and Singh, A. (2011). Influence of adjustment on academic achievement of adolescent students. *Behavioural Scientist*, 12(1), 51-56.

Parpagga, Monika (2005). Self confidence as related to parental encouragement. M.ED. Dissertation, Panjab university, Chandigarh.

Parti. R. (2012). Comparative study of adjustment of rural and urban adolescents in relation to their Parental Involvement. M. Ed Dissertation, University School of Open Learning, Panjab university Chandigarh

Parveen, Aisha (2007*). Impact of parental encouragement on emotional maturity in relation to gender and faculty'*, M.Ed. Dissertation, Panjab university, Chandigarh.

Raj Lakshmi, Aishwariya & Arora, Meenakshi (2006). *Perceived parental behaviour as related to student's academic school success and competence.* Ph.D. Psychology, Panjab university, Chandigarh.

Raju, M. A. and Samiullah, S. (2011). Impact of parental involvement on academic achievement of VII standard students. *Journal of Community Guidance and Research*, 28,(2)224-228.

Ramiah,l.(1990). A relational study of parental encouragement and academic achievement of standard 10th students in Decakottai educational district. M.Phil. Edu., Alagappa University. *Fifth Survey of Research in Education*, 24, (6) 738- 741.

Rana, S. (2012). *Study habits if 10+1 class students in relation to their socio-economic status.* M..Ed. Dissertation, Panjab university, Chandigarh.

Riaz. A, Kiran. A and Malik, N. (2002). Study habits in relation to educational achievements. *International Journal of Agriculture and Biology,* 1560–8530/2002/04–3–370–371

Rossi, A.S. (1965). Transition to parenthood. *Journal of Marriage and Family*. 30, 26-30.

Sadanandam, M. and Lourdusamy, V. (2011). Parental influence on academic achievement of higher secondary students. *Edutracks,* 11, (1)33-39.

Sakshi (2010). *Comparative study of the Parental Encouragement among the students of secondary schools in Ferozpur District*. M.Ed. Dissertation, Panjab University, Chandigarh.

Sewell.W.H, Shah.V.P (1968). Social class, parental encouragement, and educational aspirations. *American Journal of Sociology,* 73, 5(5) 59-572.

Sharma, K. P. and Sharma, V. (2011). Relationship of academic achievement of students with thinking styles. *Indian Journal of Psychometry and Education,* 42, (2)138-143.

Sharma, R.R .(1988). *Manual for Parental Encouragement Scale.* National Psychological Corporation, Agra.

Sharma, S. and Gupta, P. (2012). A study of academic performance of under graduate students in relation to their emotional intelligence. *Journal of education & Psycholoresearch,* 2(2), 46-49.

Sharma, S. and Priya (2011). Difference in academic performance and academic anxiety of rural adolescents. *Praachi Journal of Psycho-cultural dimensions.*27(1), 52-56.

Shelly (2011). Relationship among personality traits, approaches to learning, study skills and academic achievement of pharmacy students. *Journal of Community Guidance and Research,* 28,(2)229-239.

Shrama, A., Thakur, K. S., Sharma, P. and Malhotra, D. (2011). Prediction of different streams in academic achievement through verbal and non-verbal intelligence tests. *Journal of Community Guidance and Research*, 28(1), 48-55.

Shrama, M. and Khatoon, T. (2011). Family variables as predictors of students' achievement in science. *Journal of Community Guidance and Research*, 28(1), 28-36.

Shrama, M. and Khatoon, T. (2011). Family variables as predictors of students' achievement in science. *Journal of Community Guidance and Research,* 28,(1)28-36.

Sidana.A. (2013). *Problem solving ability and parental encouragement as determinant of academic achievement.* M.Ed. Dissertation Panjab University, Chandigarh.

Singaravelu, S. (2011). Emotional Intelligence and academic achievement of higher secondary students. *Behavioural Scientist (Bi-annual),* 12, (2)171-176.

Singh, K. S. (2011). Study habits in relation to anxiety and achievement. Indian *Journal of Psychometry and Education,* 42, (1)14-15.

Singh, R. (2008). Learning style preference and academic achievement of school children. *Psycho Linguistic Association of India,* 38, (1)40-47.

Singh, S. and Thukral, P. (2011). Emotional maturity and academic achievement of high school students. *Journal of Community Guidance & Research,* 28, 1089-93.

Sood, S. (2013). Study habits and attitudes of adolescents as related to parental encouragement. *Parview,* 1(2), 125-130.

Sunder, P. (2009). Academic achievement and intelligence of students of bachelor of education. *Behavioural Scientist,* 10,(2)169-172.

Sutherman, S. and Vasanthi, A. (2011). Study habits and academic achievement of 9th standard students in Palani educational district. *Edutracks,* 10, (11) 39-42.

Symonds, P.M. (1945). *The dynamics of parent-child relationship,* New York, Teacher College, Columbia University.

Thomas H. Estes and Herbert C. Richards (2012). Habits of study and test performance. *Journal of Reading Behavior 1985, XVII, (1).*

Tiwari, J. and Naithani, R. (2011). Impact of parent child relationship on scholastic achievement of adolescents. *Indian Journal of Psychometry and Education,* 42, (1)23-25.

Uniyal, M.P and Agarwal, K. (1982). *Manual for Parental Encouragement Scale,* Department of Education, Garhwal University.

Valentine, J. C., DuBois, D. L. and Cooper, H. (2004). The relation between self-beliefs and academic achievement: A meta-analytic review. *Educational Psychologist,.* 39 (2), 111-133.

Vasanthi, A. (2010) Learning Environment and academic achievement of higher secondary Physics students. *Edutracks,* 10,(1), 42-45.

Verma, B.P. and Sheikh, G. Q. (1998). Personality traits and needs as correlates of academic achievement. *Indian Journal of Psychometry and Education,* 29, (1), 65-70.

Verma, K. (2011). Academic achievement of high and low creative students. Indian *Journal of Psychometry and Education*,42, (2),189-191.

Wentzel, K. R. (1991). Relations between social competence and academic achievement in early adolescence. Child Development, 62, (5),1066–1078.

White, K. R. (1982). The relation between socioeconomic status and academic achievement. *Psychological Bulletin*, 91(3), 461-481.

White, K. R. (1982). The relation between socioeconomic status and academic achievement. *Psychological Bulletin*, 91, (3) 461-481.

William H. Sewell, Vimal P. Shah (1968). Social class, parental encouragement, and educational aspirations. *American Journal of Sociology*, 73, (5), 559-572

Yadav, S. (2012). Emotional intelligence and values of adolescents studying in govt. And non govt. Schools. *Journal of education & Psychological Research*, 2(2), 11-14.

Zolten, K. & Long. N. (1997). *Improving study habits.* Department of Pediatrics University of Arkansas. Retrieved December 29, 2013.

WEBSITES

- http://iclll2011.oum.edu.my/extfiles/pdf/Motivation%20and%20Study%20Habits%20of%20Working%20Adults%20A%20Case%20Study%20of%20Masters%20Students%20in%20Open%20University%20Malaysia.pdf
- http://ijl.cgpublisher.com/product/pub.30/prod.1502
- http://journals.upd.edu.ph/index.php/ali/article/viewFile/1769/1685
- http://psycnet.apa.org/journals/fam/26/6/927/
  http://questgarden.com/23/08/8/060419215421/index.htm
- http://tanestelle.blogspot.in/2011/02/review-of-related-literature.html
- http://tanestelle.blogspot.in/2011/03/review-of-related-literature.html
- http://www.ajol.info/index.php/ejc/article/viewFile/63610/51444/
- http://www.australia.edu/Resources/learning-good-study-habits.html

- http://www.cedu.niu.edu/~shumow/iit/Sports-Related%20Stress.pdf
- http://www.ijab.org
- http://www.ncbi.nlm.nih.gov/pmc/articles/PMC2799384/
- http://www.open-science-repository.com/study-habits-and-attitudes-the-road-to-academic-success.html
- http://www.parenting-ed.org.
- http://www.pediatricnursing.org/article/S0882-5963(00)80035-4/abstract
- http://www.pediatricnursing.org/article/S0882-5963(00)80036-6/abstract
- http://www.phoenix.edu/forward/student-life/2011/06/developing-good-study-habits.html
- http://www.ssc.wisc.edu/wlsresearch/publications/files/public/Sewell-Shah_Social.Class.Parental.Encouragement.and.Educational.Aspirations.pdf date 25/11/13
- http://www.termpaperwarehouse.com/essay-on/Related-Literature-Study-Habits/60766
- http://www.termpaperwarehouse.com/essay-on/Study-Habit/54838
- http://www.termpaperwarehouse.com/essay-on/Study-Habits/93300

www.ingramcontent.com/pod-product-compliance
Lightning Source LLC
Chambersburg PA
CBHW060417050426
42449CB00009B/2006